DENZEL WASHINGTON

The African-American Biographies Series

MARIAN ANDERSON
Singer and Humanitarian
0-7660-1211-5

LOUIS ARMSTRONG
King of Jazz
0-89490-997-5

BENJAMIN BANNEKER
Astronomer and Mathematician
0-7660-1208-5

MARY MCLEOD BETHUNE
Educator and Activist
0-7660-1771-0

JULIAN BOND
Civil Rights Activist and Chairman of
the NAACP
0-7660-1549-1

RALPH BUNCHE
Winner of the Nobel Peace Prize
0-7660-1203-4

**GEORGE WASHINGTON
CARVER**
Scientist and Inventor
0-7660-1770-2

BESSIE COLEMAN
First Black Woman Pilot
0-7660-1545-9

FREDERICK DOUGLASS
Speaking Out Against Slavery
0-7660-1773-7

DR. CHARLES DREW
Blood Bank Innovator
0-7660-2117-3

W. E. B. DU BOIS
Champion of Civil Rights
0-7660-1209-3

**PAUL LAURENCE
DUNBAR**
Portrait of a Poet
0-7660-1350-2

DUKE ELLINGTON
Giant of Jazz
0-89490-691-7

NIKKI GIOVANNI
Poet of the People
0-7660-1238-7

WHOOPI GOLDBERG
Comedian and Movie Star
0-7660-1205-0

FANNIE LOU HAMER
Fighting for the Right to Vote
0-7660-1772-9

LORRAINE HANSBERRY
Playwright and Voice of Justice
0-89490-945-2

MATTHEW HENSON
Co-Discoverer of the North Pole
0-7660-1546-7

LANGSTON HUGHES
Poet of the Harlem Renaissance
0-89490-815-4

ZORA NEALE HURSTON
Southern Storyteller
0-89490-685-2

JESSE JACKSON
Civil Rights Activist
0-7660-1390-1

MAHALIA JACKSON
The Voice of Gospel and Civil Rights
0-7660-2115-7

QUINCY JONES
Musician, Composer, Producer
0-89490-814-6

BARBARA JORDAN
Congresswoman, Lawyer,
Educator
0-89490-692-5

CORETTA SCOTT KING
Striving for Civil Rights
0-89490-811-1

**MARTIN LUTHER
KING, JR.**
Leader for Civil Rights
0-89490-687-9

JOHN LEWIS
From Freedom Rider to Congressman
0-7660-1768-0

THURGOOD MARSHALL
Civil Rights Attorney and
Supreme Court Justice
0-7660-1547-5

KWEISI MFUME
Congressman and NAACP Leader
0-7660-1237-9

TONI MORRISON
Nobel Prize-Winning Author
0-89490-688-7

WALTER DEAN MYERS
Writer for Real Teens
0-7660-1206-9

JESSE OWENS
Track and Field Legend
0-89490-812-X

COLIN POWELL
Soldier and Patriot
0-89490-810-3

A. PHILIP RANDOLPH
Union Leader and Civil Rights
Crusader
0-7660-1544-0

PAUL ROBESON
Actor, Singer, Political Activist
0-89490-944-4

JACKIE ROBINSON
Baseball's Civil Rights Legend
0-89490-690-9

BETTY SHABAZZ
Sharing the Vision
of Malcolm X
0-7660-1210-7

MARY CHURCH TERRELL
Speaking Out for Civil Rights
0-7660-2116-5

HARRIET TUBMAN
Moses of the Underground Railroad
0-7660-1548-3

MADAM C. J. WALKER
Self-Made Businesswoman
0-7660-1204-2

DENZEL WASHINGTON
Academy Award–Winning Actor
0-7660-2131-9

IDA B. WELLS-BARNETT
Crusader Against Lynching
0-89490-947-9

OPRAH WINFREY
Talk Show Legend
0-7660-1207-7

CARTER G. WOODSON
Father of African-American History
0-89490-946-0

RICHARD WRIGHT
Author of *Native Son* and *Black Boy*
0-7660-1769-9

—African-American Biographies—

DENZEL WASHINGTON

Academy Award–Winning Actor

Series Consultant:
Dr. Russell L. Adams, Chairman
Department of Afro-American Studies, Howard University

Sara McIntosh Wooten

Enslow Publishers, Inc.

40 Industrial Road	PO Box 38
Box 398	Aldershot
Berkeley Heights, NJ 07922	Hants GU12 6BP
USA	UK

http://www.enslow.com

Library of Congress Cataloging-in-Publication Data

Wooten, Sara McIntosh.
    Denzel Washington : Academy Award-winning actor / Sara McIntosh Wooten.
        p. cm. — (African-American biographies)
    Summary: A biography of the African American actor who earned a historic second Academy Award in 2002 for his portrayal of Detective Alonzo Harris in the movie "Training Day."
    Includes bibliographical references and index.
    ISBN 0-7660-2131-9
    1. Washington, Denzel, 1954– —Juvenile literature. 2. Actors—United States—Biography—Juvenile literature. 3. African American actors—United States—Biography—Juvenile literature. [1. Washington, Denzel, 1954– 2. Actors and actresses. 3. African Americans—Biography.] I. Title. II. Series.
PN2287.W452 W66   2003
791.43'028'092—dc21

                                 2002152975

Printed in the United States of America

10 9 8 7 6 5 4 3 2 1

To Our Readers: We have done our best to make sure all Internet Addresses in this book were active and appropriate when we went to press. However, the author and the publisher have no control over and assume no liability for the material available on those Internet sites or on other Web sites they may link to. Any comments or suggestions can be sent by e-mail to comments@enslow.com or to the address on the back cover.

Every effort has been made to locate all copyright holders of material used in this book. If any errors or omissions have occurred, corrections will be made in future editions of this book.

Illustration Credits: Boys and Girls Clubs of America, pp. 22, 105; Courtesy Everett Collection, pp. 6, 10, 14, 30, 39, 45, 48, 54, 59, 62, 73, 81, 83, 90, 97, 100, 109.

Cover Illustration: Photofest

CONTENTS

Playing a bad guy in the movie *Training Day* turned out to be good luck for actor Denzel Washington.

1

At the Top

nd the winner is . . . Denzel Washington!"
With the roar of applause pounding in
his ears, a beaming Denzel Washington
approached the podium to accept the award for Best
Actor at the 2002 Academy Awards ceremony. He had
earned the film industry's highest recognition for his
role as Detective Sergeant Alonzo Harris in the movie
Training Day. With that, Washington made Hollywood
history as the first African American to win two
Academy Awards.

Washington's triumph helped break a long trend
that seemed to favor awards for white actors.

Washington was not the first African American to be named Best Actor. But it had been thirty-nine years since Sidney Poitier's win for his performance in *Lilies of the Field*.

The power of an Academy Award is huge. For an actor, it can be a life-changing event, leading to increased recognition and respect—and more roles. At the box office, it can mean millions of dollars in added ticket sales.

The award winners are elected beforehand by the members of the Academy of Motion Picture Arts and Sciences, an organization of leaders in the filmmaking community. The results are closely guarded until their announcement on awards night. The yearly ceremony has become the entertainment industry's biggest event. Steeped in glamour and glitz, it is seen by one billion television viewers worldwide.[1]

After all the anticipation, what do the winners take home? A small gold statuette of a man, called an Oscar. The statuette itself is not expensive, but an Oscar can be priceless to its recipients.

Despite the excitement that surrounds the Academy Awards, many people in the movie industry had grown increasingly unhappy with the winning choices in recent years. There had been a clear lack of African-American nominees and winners. By 2002, only six African Americans had won an Oscar in the academy's seventy-four-year history, and five of them were for supporting roles: Hattie McDaniel (*Gone With the Wind*, 1939), Louis Gossett, Jr. (*An Officer and a Gentleman*, 1982), Whoopi Goldberg (*Ghost*, 1985), Denzel Washington (*Glory*, 1989), and Cuba Gooding, Jr. (*Jerry Maguire*, 1996). The only Best Actor award won by a black actor had gone to Sidney Poitier (*Lilies of the Field*, 1963).

As the evening approached, Washington kept his perspective. "I just hope, when the time comes, we will all be able to be judged fairly on our work and not let our color help or hurt us," he said.[2]

As it turned out, the 2002 results reversed the trend for African Americans. First, actress Halle Berry made history when she became the first African-American woman to receive the Academy Award for Best Actress. She won for her performance in *Monster's Ball*.

The Best Actor award was then presented to Washington by one of his friends, the actress Julia Roberts. It had been a tight race, surrounded by speculation. His closest contender was thought to be Russell Crowe, who played Dr. John Nash in *A Beautiful Mind*.

Washington was used to Academy Award nominations. This was his fifth. His single win had been in 1989, when he received the award for Best Supporting Actor for his performance as a runaway slave in the movie *Glory*.

So Washington knew what to expect at the awards

And the winner is . . . Best Actor Denzel Washington and Best Actress Halle Berry made history at the Academy Awards ceremony in 2002.

ceremony. He certainly was not counting on winning the big one that night. In fact, his wife had to nudge him away from the television set to go to the ceremony. He was caught up in watching the NCAA (National College Athletic Association) basketball finals. Deeply religious, Washington also read from the Bible before setting out for the evening. Win or lose, he told his four children, the family would celebrate when he got home.

The part of Alonzo Harris in *Training Day* had been a dramatic departure for Washington. Over his twenty-one-year film career, he had become known mainly for playing heroic roles in films such as *Courage Under Fire* (1996), *The Siege* (1998), and *Remember the Titans* (2000). This had been his first attempt at playing a full-fledged "bad guy."

Training Day takes place in one twenty-four-hour period. It is set in the rough world of south Los Angeles, California. The streets are infested with gangs, drugs, and violence. As Alonzo Harris, Washington plays a corrupt undercover narcotics cop who dresses in black and wears heavy silver chains and a tattoo reading "Death is certain. Life is not." *Training Day* audiences knew immediately that this was not a typical Denzel Washington part.

In the movie, Harris is joined by rookie cop Jake Hoyt, played by actor Ethan Hawke. Hoyt craves the excitement and challenge of being a narcotics cop.

If he can hold his own with Harris during this day of training, he can move forward with his career.

As Alonzo Harris, Washington improvised many of his lines, making them up as the movie was filmed. With his fast-paced dialogue, he controls the scenes as Jake, along with the audience, ping-pongs back and forth between shock, amusement, assurance, and terror.

To keep in character, Washington made a note on his script: "The wages of sin [are] death." Later he said, "Every time I looked at those words, I felt like I could be as wicked as I wanted to be, because I knew what was coming . . . for Alonzo. I think it's good to get a bad guy in there to mix up my image."[3]

Although Washington's performance was highly praised, some moviegoers were less than pleased with the film's brutality and violence. Others were disturbed by Washington's change in character. Was Washington himself concerned with audience reactions? "No," he said. "Every movie I've done, I've done because I wanted to. Not because I thought [about what] people were going to think of it. . . . There'll be people that won't like me in this. It's their decision. There's people who don't like me as the good guy."[4]

The Academy Award for Best Actor is seldom given to an actor for playing a villain. By 2002, it had been ten years since Anthony Hopkins won for his terrifying role in the film *Silence of the Lambs*.

"I guess in this case being bad has been good to me. . . . I guess being the bad guy was a change, but I look at it in terms of the quality of the material," Washington said about his nomination.[5]

Earlier that evening, Washington had been onstage at the Academy Awards ceremony for a different reason. He had been chosen to present an Honorary Academy Award to his hero, the seventy-five-year-old actor Sidney Poitier. Considering Washington's win later in the evening, it was a particularly fitting choice. Poitier's acting career had forged the path for Washington and other African-American actors.[6]

As the first African American to play serious, dignified roles in movies that would be seen by mainstream audiences, Poitier broke away from the stereotyped roles normally reserved for black actors. He became most well known and admired for his performances in *Lilies of the Field* (1963), *To Sir With Love* (1967), *Guess Who's Coming to Dinner?* (1967), and *In the Heat of the Night* (1967). From acting, Poitier went on to produce and direct films.

In his tribute to Poitier that night, Washington credited him for his "body of work, influence on the industry, and work to better the industry." Later, when Washington was accepting his award for Best Actor, he pointed to Poitier's leadership, saying, "For forty years I've been chasing Sidney. I'll always be following in his footsteps."[7]

Actor Sidney Poitier has been a role model and an inspiration to Denzel Washington.

Indeed, it had been Poitier who gave Washington wise advice when he was just beginning to evaluate movie scripts. He told Washington, "Son, your first three or four films will dictate how you are viewed your entire career. Choose wisely, follow your gut and wait it out if you can."[8]

It had not been easy. Early in his career, Washington was offered roles that would have provided a much-needed paycheck—but would have meant playing parts he considered demeaning for an African American. He took Poitier's advice. It eventually paid off, leading to his success as an actor.

Today, Washington is considered one of Hollywood's biggest box office draws. He is also one of the few African-American actors who can attract mass audiences of all races. He has proved that he can cross racial boundaries and play parts intended for white actors. He has become known and respected for the extensive research and preparation he brings to his roles. Drawing top salary, Washington makes up to $20 million for a movie.

After the 2002 Academy Awards ceremony, Denzel Washington went home to celebrate with his family. As he left that evening, many in the audience knew little of the long and difficult path he had followed to reach that pinnacle.

2

A Strong Beginning

enzel Washington was born on December 28, 1954, in Mount Vernon, New York. He was named for his father, Denzel senior, a Pentecostal minister who had moved to New York from his family home in Virginia. Denzel's mother, Lennis, was born in Georgia and raised in Harlem. She now worked as a beautician. Denzel was the second of three children. He had an older sister, Lorice, and later a younger brother, David.

Denzel was born at a time when the nation was divided by race. In the mid-1950s, whites were looking forward to growing economic stability and prosperity.

The country still proudly remembered its victory with the Allies in World War II. New technology was developing, and industry was expanding at an ever-increasing pace. Products like television sets and dishwashers would soon be commonplace in American homes. At the same time, houses were becoming more affordable and car production was skyrocketing. With personal and national prosperity, the future looked bright for many.[1]

But the picture was quite different for most African Americans. Regardless of whether they lived in the North or the South, they faced segregation—racial separation—everywhere they turned. Their lives were limited to blacks-only neighborhoods, restaurants, hotels, and schools. Facilities for African Americans were almost always substandard to those for whites. Housing for most African Americans was overcrowded, badly built, and poorly maintained. To better their futures, they needed good jobs, but job opportunities for African Americans were mainly limited to menial labor at very low pay.

The major national push for civil rights, led by Martin Luther King, Jr., and others, was still a decade away. Years of struggle and discord lay ahead before the general society would become desegregated. In the 1950s, the American dream was for whites only.

Against that backdrop, Mount Vernon, New York, was an unusual community. Located about thirty minutes north of New York City, Mount Vernon was home to mostly middle-class people of varying cultures and races who lived side-by-side in relative peace.

Growing up, Denzel had friends from diverse backgrounds—Irish, Italian, and West Indian, as well as African-American. It was an enriching environment. Years later, visiting Mount Vernon, Denzel fondly remembered his childhood, saying, "Growing up there was a wonderful time in my life."[2]

The Washingtons were determined to build a strong family foundation. They were strict parents with high expectations. Denzel described it as a "motivated, hard-working family."[3]

His parents began by setting personal examples for their children. Both worked very hard at their jobs. Besides his ministry, the Reverend Washington held two other jobs, one at a local department store and the other in the Mount Vernon water department. With their father's heavy work schedule, the Washington children rarely saw him. He left before they got up in the morning and arrived home after they went to bed at night. Because of that, he and Denzel never developed a close relationship.[4] Even so, Denzel had an abiding respect for his father and appreciated the effort he made to build a strong family.[5]

Denzel's mother also had high demands on her time and energy. She owned and operated the beauty parlor in which she worked as a beautician. Over time she would expand her business to include several beauty parlors. Denzel remembers her influence—she set the tone in the house. "I owe her everything," he would say years later.[6]

The Washingtons ran a disciplined household. Smoking, drinking alcohol, and swearing were forbidden. The children were rarely allowed to see movies. When they did, they were limited to Disney animations or religious epics like *The Ten Commandments*.

Religion was always a core family value and remains so for Denzel. He has attributed his deep, enduring religious faith to keeping him grounded amid the glitter of his celebrity.[7] "[My father] and my mother gave me a moral center that has never gone away," he said.[8]

Today Washington recognizes the secure anchor his parents gave him with their high expectations and tight control. He looks back on his family with pride, describing his upbringing as "strict" and "tough." "But it was good."[9] The lessons he learned from his parents—the value of hard work and devotion to family—set the course for the way he has lived his life.

When Denzel was just six years old, he began going to the nearby Mount Vernon Boys Club (now part of the Boys and Girls Clubs of America). Located in an old two-story building, it was a good place for neighborhood boys to go after school and on Saturdays. There, they could get together with friends, play sports, and just hang out. Sometimes they organized camping trips. And the Boys Club counselors gave Denzel and his friends someone to talk to.

Denzel's friends from that time remember him as shy. He had a gap between his two front teeth that caused him some embarrassment. Despite that, he was popular with the girls because of his good looks.[10] Guys liked him because he was a good athlete and fun to be around.[11]

Denzel was only an average student in elementary school. But he thrived at the Boys Club. Through its sports program he learned to play football and basketball. Some of his friendships with the boys and counselors there would last for years. More than that, he got the guidance and encouragement to make the most of his life. Years later Washington credited the Boys Club by saying, "Everything you've seen or heard about me, in the media and in the movies, began with lessons I learned to live by at the Club."[12] The Boys Club would become his home away from home until he left for college.

Denzel began working at a local barbershop when he was twelve years old, doing odd jobs, running errands for clients, and sweeping the floor. He loved making money, later saying, "Everybody looked like a dollar bill to me."[13] Earning his own spending money helped Denzel develop a sense of independence and pride.[14]

Young Denzel was an enthusiastic member of the Boys Club of Mount Vernon football team.

But trouble loomed for the Washington family. When Denzel was fourteen years old, his parents separated. Eventually they divorced. His father moved back to Virginia, and the family had little contact with him after that. Now his mother was alone, with full responsibility for the three children.

It was a tough time for Denzel. He was angry and confused and began to hang out with kids who were getting into trouble. But Denzel did not care. It gave him a way to express his frustration and disappointment with his family situation.[15]

Despite running with a bad crowd, Denzel never got arrested. He attributes that to a combination of luck and his family upbringing. Some of his friends were not as lucky. Several eventually served time in prison.[16]

Ever watchful of her children, Lennis Washington was disturbed by the direction her son's life was taking. She knew he was spending time with the wrong crowd and was afraid he would get into serious trouble. Despite her limited funds, she wanted to send Denzel to a private boarding school. The Oakland Academy was about an hour away, in New Windsor, New York. Denzel was accepted by the prestigious school and given a partial scholarship.

Oakland Academy provided a disciplined, structured environment with an emphasis on academic achievement to prepare its students for college. This all-boys school with only about one hundred students was a big change for Denzel. For one thing, he lived at the school, going home only for holidays and some weekends. In addition, most of the other students there were white and wealthy.

At Oakland, Denzel was more interested in sports than academics. He did not study as much as he could have, and his grades suffered. He enjoyed playing football, baseball, and basketball, though, and was a strong competitor.[17] He even dreamed of becoming a professional athlete some day.[18]

After four years at Oakland, Denzel graduated in 1972. His future was still a big question. He knew he would go to college; that had always been his mother's expectation for him. But where? His grades were not high enough to win a scholarship to Boston University, his first choice. So he enrolled at nearby Fordham University. Located in New York City, Fordham is a Jesuit university offering a strong liberal arts education. Once that decision was made, though, Denzel had no idea what career to pursue. He still had some searching to do before he would discover the path that would lead him to fame and fortune.

3

THE START OF SOMETHING BIG

t Fordham, Washington first decided to pursue a career in medicine. But premedical studies did not turn out to be the right direction for him. For one thing, he quickly found that some of the science courses were over his head. "I could not only not say the name of one of the courses I had to take—chordaemorphogenesis—but I definitely couldn't pass it," he said.[1]

Soon Washington got into the habit of skipping classes. And once he got behind in his studies, it was hard to catch up. Not surprisingly, his grades fell. He finished his freshman year with a dismal academic showing.

By the end of the first semester of his sophomore year, Washington was still floundering. His college career seemed doomed. He decided to take a leave of absence from school. Maybe if he got some work experience in the real world, he would find the direction he so desperately needed.[2]

Washington spent the next nine months trying to pull his life together. He worked for the post office for a while. Then he worked as a garbage collector for the New York City sanitation department. Neither job satisfied him. He even thought about joining the army. He began to realize that to have the life he wanted, he must return to Fordham and complete his college education.[3]

That summer Washington got another job—this time as a counselor at a YMCA camp in Lakeville, Connecticut. He was hired to supervise sports and help organize camp talent shows. As one of the camp activities, the counselors put on a play for the campers. It was an event that marked the beginning of a change in Washington's life.

To his surprise, he found that performing onstage came naturally to him. For someone with little exposure to acting and movies as a child, Washington's ease as a performer was all the more amazing. Not only did he feel comfortable, his sense of presence and his confidence were transmitted to the audience as well.[4] Both counselors and campers were struck with his ability, and they let him know. Suddenly, he was getting positive feedback. It was a welcome relief after the previous two years of confusion and failure.

At the end of the summer, Washington returned to Fordham. His favorite freshman course had been Introduction to Communications, a class on writing and public speaking. Based on that experience, he decided to change his major from premed to journalism. In addition to his studies, he continued playing baseball, basketball, and football.

The following summer, remembering his success at the YMCA camp the year before, Washington enrolled in a drama workshop. It was taught by Robinson Stone, a Fordham professor of English and dramatic literature. Stone was also a professional actor who had appeared in various productions, including the 1953 award-winning *Stalag 17*, a movie about American soldiers in a German prisoner-of-war camp during World War II.

During the workshop, Washington began to learn the basics of stage acting. Sure enough, he found the same sense of comfort and rightness that he had felt the year before. "At last," he said later, "something was exciting to me. It was like I had found my niche. Suddenly, college took on a new meaning."[5]

Stone was quick to recognize Washington's talent. Over time, he would become a mentor to Washington and help him toward his career.

With a growing sense of confidence in his acting ability, Washington began his junior year at Fordham in the fall of 1975. In addition to journalism, he added drama as a major field of study. Where some might see the fields as unrelated, Washington saw a close link. He believed that an effective actor has to study and research his roles, just as an investigative reporter pursues a story. Years later, he still held that view: "To play a part, I get with real people and find out how they feel and think and live, which is much like what a reporter does."[6] Washington's diligence and thoroughness in preparing for a part would become one of his trademarks, as well as one of the reasons for his success.

That year the Fordham drama department was doing *The Emperor Jones*, a play by Eugene O'Neill. The main character, Brutus Jones, escapes from a chain gang and eventually becomes the king of Haiti. Washington auditioned for and won the title role. He was outstanding in the part. Stone was so impressed he called Washington "the best actor [he] had seen onstage."[7]

By this time, Washington was hooked. As he later said, "I enjoyed learning the lines. I enjoyed being out in front of people. I enjoyed the way they responded to me. Then someone said to me, 'You can do this for a living.'"[8] Washington began to agree.

During his senior year at Fordham, Washington landed another big part—the title role in William

Shakespeare's *Othello*. The drama centers on Othello's belief that he has been betrayed by a close friend. Shakespeare wrote the part of Othello to be played by a black man; Othello's wife, Desdemona, is white. The issue of race lurks just beneath the story's plot.

The play has been performed countless times by actors far more experienced and accomplished than Denzel Washington was at that time. It is a difficult role for an actor, requiring passion, discipline, and a majestic presence.[9]

Despite the challenge, Washington's performance went beyond his training. He showed originality in his interpretation. In one scene, in which a desperate and frustrated Othello usually screams his lines, Washington took a different approach. He delivered the lines in a whisper. It showed his ability to go beyond the norm to create a fresh character portrayal.[10]

The result? Audiences loved him. In an interview, Washington reflected on his success playing Othello: "I got excellent feedback right from the start, which was a determining factor in my career."[11]

Again, Stone was delighted with his student's ability. He invited several talent agents to watch Washington's performance. Before long, Washington had signed with the William Morris Agency and landed his first role as a professional actor.

Washington was cast in the television movie *Wilma*. It was about the life of African-American athlete Wilma

Rudolph. She had overcome polio as a child and went on to win three gold medals in track and field at the 1960 Olympics. In the movie, Cicely Tyson played Wilma Rudolph. Washington was cast as Wilma's boyfriend, Robert Eldridge, whom she later married.

While filming *Wilma*, Washington found performing before a camera to be quite different from the stage acting he was used to. There was no audience to play to and get feedback from. Instead, only a camera recorded his performance. The director had to coach

In his first professional role, Washington played the boyfriend of Wilma Rudolph, shown here at the 1960 Olympics.

him to keep his head up so his face and his lines would not be lost to the camera's eye.[12]

The movie aired in 1977, the same year Washington graduated from Fordham. By this time his grades had shot up, despite the demands of a double major in drama and journalism. It was yet another sign that he had indeed found his true direction.

With *Wilma*, Washington's career was off to a promising start. By landing a role in a television movie so early in his career, Washington's future already looked bright. Yet he would find the road ahead to be more challenging than it appeared. *Wilma* did not skyrocket him to fame. Instead, years of struggle lay ahead. Still, the television movie did have one major and long-lasting impact on his life. It was on the set of *Wilma* that he met Pauletta Pearson.

4

SLOW GOING

The first day Washington began filming for *Wilma*, he had a passing conversation with one of the other actors in the movie. A North Carolina native, Pauletta Pearson had moved to New York after completing graduate school. She was an accomplished singer, actor, and classical pianist. She was playing the role of Mae Faggs, a runner and close friend of Wilma Rudolph's. She and Washington chatted briefly and then parted ways. Washington was just beginning to film his scenes; Pearson had finished hers.

The couple would not see each other again for a

year. Washington had plans to leave New York. He had been accepted by the American Conservatory Theater (ACT) in San Francisco, California. He would soon be on his way there to begin studies. The ACT is a highly respected training ground for actors. Founded in 1965, it has an international reputation for excellence. Other famous actors have been among its students, including Danny Glover, Annette Bening, and Winona Ryder.

The ACT is very selective of its students. Washington was one of the forty-five applicants accepted that year out of thousands of hopefuls. He had come a long way from five years before when poor grades limited his choices.

Students at the ACT followed an intensive three-year course of study. The program included classes on acting techniques, dancing, and set design. In addition to his classes, Washington worked in a restaurant to earn money for expenses. It was a clever choice. He knew if he worked at a restaurant, he could get free meals.

During Washington's first year at the ACT, he became increasingly restless. He began his old habit of skipping classes. He had been studying in a college environment for more than five years. Now he was eager to get out and start acting.[1]

The ACT wanted him to stay in its program. Only twenty students in Washington's class were invited to continue into their second year. Washington was one of them. But he knew he was ready to move on.

The idea of acting in movies had not been a goal of his.[2] But he was in California, so why not give it a try? In Los Angeles, Washington soon found the competition stiff. Too many actors were vying for a limited number of parts. Washington decided it was time to head back to New York—back to the world of the theater, where he was more comfortable.

In New York, Washington moved in with his mother in her Mount Vernon apartment to save on expenses. Then he began the grueling and frustrating search for work onstage. "I wanted to play Shakespeare, play the great classic roles," he later said.[3] He was one of the thousands of hopeful actors in New York.

By 1978, new civil rights laws were in place, and racist attitudes were slowly changing. Over time, job opportunities were improving for African Americans. The trend carried over to the acting profession as well, with new roles opening up for African-American actors. Before the 1960s, roles for African-American actors had been scarce. And the few that were available were almost always for stereotypical parts such as servants or criminals. In addition, theater was geared to white audiences and their interests. Plays about African Americans simply were not produced. It was discouraging for the many highly talented African-American actors and playwrights of the time.

But all that began to change in the 1960s. With the emerging civil rights movement and a growing appreciation for their culture, African Americans in the theater began to unite. They raised money to start several new theater groups. One of the most prominent was the Negro Ensemble Company (NEC). Its goal was to promote black actors, as well as plays written by African Americans about issues specific to African-American culture.[4] The growth in stage roles for African Americans would help Washington as he began to build his career.

Soon after returning to New York, Washington was invited to a friend's party. As it happened, the friend also knew Pauletta Pearson and had invited her, too. Washington did not remember Pauletta from the set of *Wilma* the year before.[5] But she remembered him, and at the party that night their friendship took off.

The very next night, Washington attended an off-Broadway play. He found his seat and got settled. At intermission, when the lights came up, he found to his amazement that once again, his path and Pearson's had crossed. She was sitting in the seat next to his.

Some of Pearson's friends were performing in the play, and she was invited to the cast party afterward. Pearson asked Washington to come along to the party. Washington gallantly suggested that they take a cab.

He was planning to treat her to the ride. The problem was, he did not know the party was some distance away. With every mile, the ride got more expensive. By the time they got to the party, Pearson had to help with the cab fare. "There went my food money for the next week," she later laughed. "But I still liked his style!"[6]

As she reminisced years later about their blossoming relationship, Pearson said, "I thought he was cute, but I fell in love with his spirit."[7] Washington was struck from the beginning, too: "I was in love with her almost from our first evening out together."[8] From then on, their friendship continued to grow. Before long, Pearson came to live with Washington in his mother's apartment.

Meanwhile, Washington's auditions began to get results. Over the next year, he won parts in several off-Broadway plays and costarred in a television movie, *Flesh and Blood* (1979). Still, he was not making enough money as an actor to support himself. To make ends meet, he became a regular in the welfare lines, along with many other out-of-work New Yorkers. He wanted to move out of his mother's apartment with Pearson, but without a stable income, they were not yet able to start a life on their own.

Over time, Washington became discouraged and troubled about his career. He was ready to quit acting altogether. He knew he was a good actor, but parts were hard to get. Even when he landed one, the work did not pay very much. Often, after spending time and energy in preparation and learning his lines, the play did not last very long. It was a desperate way to live. He found himself always wondering if a part would pan out, and where his next paycheck was coming from.[9]

Washington needed a steady paycheck—something he could depend on. It just did not seem possible as an actor. So he applied for and got a job with the local recreation department. He would be helping children with drama and sports. Denzel Washington thought his acting career was almost over.[10]

But Pearson did not think Washington should give up. She encouraged him to keep auditioning, and he did. Just one week before he was to report for work at his new job, he got a part that would keep him in acting after all. He was chosen to play Malcolm X in an off-Broadway production of *When the Chickens Come Home to Roost*, by Laurence Holder.

Malcolm X was an African-American civil rights activist of the 1950s and 1960s. He was assassinated in 1965 at the age of thirty-nine. A controversial figure during much of his life, he advocated black supremacy. This philosophy said that the black race was superior to the white race.

Washington did not know the details of Malcolm X's life when he was chosen for this role. His parents had not agreed with Malcolm's extreme ideas.

Malcolm X, right, was one of the most controversial activists of the civil rights movement.

So Washington set out to learn all he could about Malcolm X in preparation for the role. He read widely and watched videos of Malcolm X's speeches. He dyed his hair red to look the part. He wanted to make the most of this opportunity.

The play consisted of a fictional confrontation between Malcolm X and Elijah Muhammad. Muhammad was the leader of the Nation of Islam, the religion to which Malcolm X was devoted. The two men had been at odds toward the end of Malcolm's life, and many suspected Muhammad of having ordered Malcolm's assassination.

When the Chickens Come Home to Roost turned out to be the career opportunity that Washington had been longing for. The play itself was a financial disappointment and closed after only twelve shows, but Washington's talent was finally noticed. African Americans who had known Malcolm X were amazed at Washington's realistic portrayal of the slain civil rights leader. Some even called his widow, Betty Shabazz, urging her to see the play. She refused, saying that it would be too difficult emotionally for her.[11]

Washington's performance received praise from New York theater critics. He also received an Audelco Award for his outstanding portrayal. Audelco is short for Audience Development Committee, an organization committed to promoting African-American theater and the arts.

By the time *Chickens* closed, Washington had a deep feeling that he would play the character of Malcolm X again one day.[12] It would take eleven years for his prediction to come true. But first, his acting career would take him in many other directions.

5

PICKING UP SPEED

ust two weeks after *When the Chickens Come Home to Roost* closed, Washington began rehearsals for another big part. He was cast as Private First Class Melvin Peterson in *A Soldier's Play*, by Charles Fuller. The murder mystery takes place at Fort Neal, an army base in Louisiana. The fictional setting is home to an African-American company of soldiers serving under white commanders during World War II.

Racial tension is an undercurrent throughout the play—not only between whites and blacks, but among the black soldiers themselves. When an

African-American drill sergeant is murdered, the tension explodes.

A Soldier's Play was produced off Broadway by the Negro Ensemble Company. It was hugely successful, praised by audiences and critics alike. The drama won several awards, including the Outer Critics Circle Award for Best Off-Broadway Play and the New York Drama Critics Circle Award for Best American Play. Later it won a Pulitzer Prize, one of the highest honors for a literary work.

Washington's performance was also praised. He received an Obie Award, an honor for excellence in an off-Broadway production.

Next, Washington won his first movie role, in *Carbon Copy*, a comedy aimed at racial stereotypes. He was cast as the result of a national talent search, after he was spotted performing in New York. In the movie, Washington plays Roger Porter, a seventeen-year-old high school student who claims to be the illegitimate son of a wealthy white businessman. That part is played by George Segal (seen more recently as Jack Gallo in the television comedy *Just Shoot Me*).

Washington had high hopes that this national movie would be the break he needed to secure his career, but he was wrong. Neither reviewers nor the public liked the movie, and it bombed at the box office. Washington found himself back in the unemployment lines.[1]

Still, *Carbon Copy* yielded an unexpected bonus. One person who saw the movie was television producer Bruce Paltrow (father of actress Gwyneth Paltrow). At the time, he was looking for an actor to play a supporting role in a television series he would be producing soon.

The new show, *St. Elsewhere*, would take place in a fictional Boston hospital called St. Eligius. Paltrow wanted Washington to play Dr. Phillip Chandler. Other doctors on the show would be played by such actors as Howie Mandel and Ed Begley, Jr. William Daniels, who later starred as Mr. Feeney in the television comedy *Boy Meets World*, was also cast in the drama.

Instead of leaping at this opportunity, Washington hesitated. For one thing, it would mean filming in Los Angeles. That would take him away from New York and Pauletta Pearson. He was also concerned that the role would limit his career. He did not want to be stereotyped as a TV actor. That could hamper his ability to expand into other roles.

On the other hand, the idea of playing an African-American doctor appealed to Washington. His character might help viewers begin to see African Americans in a new way. Washington also knew that filming *St. Elsewhere* episodes would not take all of his time. He would be able to work on other projects when the show was not in production.

At any rate, Washington thought the show would

probably run for only thirteen weeks before it was canceled. And for that time, he would have a steady income. So he agreed to take the part.[2]

St. Elsewhere began airing in the fall of 1982 on NBC. The episodes revolved around life in a gritty, realistic hospital and the personal dramas of some of the staff. Often the episodes dealt with difficult ethical questions. The producers wanted their series not only to entertain viewers but also to challenge them to think.

St. Elsewhere lasted for the next six years. Although its audience was relatively small, the show was critically acclaimed for breaking new ground in television. During its run, *St. Elsewhere* received twelve Emmy Awards for excellence. The show also gave Washington national exposure.

The next year, with *St. Elsewhere* providing financial security, Washington finally decided to ask Pearson to marry him. Nervous, he could only work up the courage to propose by telephone from Los Angeles.[3] A June wedding followed in Pearson's hometown of Newton, North Carolina.

Back in New York after their wedding, the couple had no time for a honeymoon. Both were too busy with their jobs. Besides filming *St. Elsewhere* episodes, Washington was still performing in *A Soldier's Play* in New York and later in Chicago.

The year 1984 brought a new life role for

Critics praised Denzel Washington's portrayal of Dr. Phillip
Chandler in *St. Elsewhere.*

Washington when his first son, John David, was born. Pauletta put her career on hold for a time to be home with their baby. For Denzel, too, becoming a father profoundly affected his perspective on his life and his career. He later reflected on this change—on his decision to be a hands-on dad: "When my first child was born it was clear where my commitment was going to be. You can't tell your kid, 'Sorry, I can't raise you now—I have a career.'"[4]

That year, in addition to his ongoing role in *St. Elsewhere*, Washington was cast in the television movie *License to Kill*. He played an assistant district attorney prosecuting a drunk driver. On top of that, the successful *A Soldier's Play* had been adapted into a movie script. Washington was again chosen to play Private Peterson. The film *A Soldier's Story* was released the same year.

It had not been easy to get the movie approved for filming. Despite acclaim for the play, producers worried about its success as a movie. It had been seventeen years since the film *In the Heat of the Night* with Sidney Poitier and Carroll O'Connor. That award-winning movie had addressed racism at the height of America's civil rights movement. Since then, attention had turned away from films about racism that were directed at white audiences. A different kind of African-American film had emerged. Movies like *Shaft* (1971) and *Superfly* (1972) featured African Americans in tough action roles and targeted black audiences. They had proved to be big moneymakers.[5] *A Soldier's Story* would not be that kind of movie at all. Producers did not know if it would attract audiences.

A Soldier's Story was finally approved, though it was given a very low budget. It was filmed at Fort Chaffee, Arkansas, in just fifty-four days. Carefully marketed, the movie was seen by a moderate audience. Still, because of its low budget, it did result in a good profit.

Critics were restrained in their praise of the movie. Most preferred the theater version. Though Washington played a supporting role, he received special notice from critics. They universally applauded his performance as skillful.[6]

After *A Soldier's Story*, Washington turned once again to television. He played the lead role in the television movie *The George McKenna Story*, which aired in 1986. It is the true story of McKenna, the principal at George Washington High School in inner-city Los Angeles. The school was known as a crime-infested haven for gangs. McKenna took on the challenge, tackling its problems of delinquency, uninterested parents and teachers, violence, and drugs. Under McKenna's leadership, the school was transformed into a safe, structured environment where students earned national academic honors.

Also in 1986 Washington had a small but important part in the movie *Power*. Richard Gere stars in this

In the movie *A Soldier's Story*, Washington recreated his award-winning off-Broadway role as an army private in World War II.

exploration of the corrupt side of national politics. Washington plays Arnold Billings, a political lobbyist who works behind the scenes to control politicians and their careers. It was the first time Washington played a part that had been written for a white man.[7]

The role appealed to Washington because it was a switch from typical African-American stereotypes.[8] Even though he was corrupt, Billings was also wealthy, sophisticated, and successful. Unfortunately, *Power* met with disappointment at the box office. Reviewers called it a predictable handling of an old and overused theme.

By the end of 1986, eight years had passed since Washington left San Francisco to make a living as an actor. In that time he had gone from standing in welfare lines to receiving critical acclaim in theater, film, and television. He would find that this success was just the beginning.

6

THE FAST TRACK

n 1986, Sir Richard Attenborough was planning a movie about life in South Africa. Attenborough is a well-known actor and director. He had won an Academy Award for Best Picture in 1982 for the movie *Gandhi*, which he produced and directed. Now he wanted to address the issue of apartheid in South Africa.

Apartheid was the legalized system of racial segregation (separation) in South Africa, where it was a long-established way of life. By law, blacks could live only in certain areas of the country. Their homes were shacks with few modern conveniences. Travel was restricted for blacks, as well. They had to carry government-issued permits. On top of that, jobs and education for blacks were strictly controlled by white laws.

Attenborough, like many others, was outraged by apartheid. He wanted to make a major motion picture about the subject to bring it to the world's attention.

Attenborough's script was based on the life of Stephen Biko, a black South African activist who crusaded against apartheid. Biko was arrested because of his views and was killed in prison in 1977.

The story Attenborough wanted to film also included a fifth-generation white South African newspaper editor named Donald Woods. Like most South Africans, Woods had been raised to be a white supremacist. He used his newspaper to condemn efforts to change the apartheid system. Then, in 1965, he met Stephen Biko, who convinced Woods that his beliefs were wrong. With Biko's help, Woods began to look at South Africa from the black viewpoint. The two men became close friends, and Woods started to work actively against apartheid.

When Biko was murdered, Woods wanted the truth of his death and the brutality of apartheid to receive worldwide attention. He hoped that the South African government would then be forced to change its laws. So he decided to write a book about Biko's life.

The South African government did not want Biko's

story told. It placed Woods under house arrest and restricted his activities. He was banned from writing. Still, Woods persevered, and friends smuggled his manuscript, chapter by chapter, out of South Africa to England. Finally, Woods and his family fled South Africa altogether. They left their home and friends behind in order to escape further government persecution.

Attenborough hoped to cast a South African actor as Stephen Biko, but no one who auditioned seemed right for the part. After seeing Washington in *A Soldier's Story* and talking to him in person, Attenborough felt he had found his Biko. Actor Kevin Kline would play Biko's friend Donald Woods.

The movie ran into trouble from the start. Attenborough was criticized because the focus was split between Biko and Woods. Many thought it would be more powerful to spotlight Biko alone. But Attenborough held firm, saying that he would not be able to get the movie funded, or attract the audiences he wanted, without including Donald Woods's story.[1]

Washington himself was not convinced that he should take the part. It would mean being in Africa, far from his family, for several months. He, too, was troubled by the movie's split focus. But realizing the importance of both stories, he decided to go ahead: "The important thing to me was to give people a chance to find out who [Biko] is. . . ."[2]

Cry Freedom was shot in Zimbabwe, a country neighboring South Africa. To prepare, Washington immersed himself in tapes of Biko's speeches to learn more about the man and his beliefs. He also needed to imitate the way Biko talked. That meant learning to speak with Biko's South African accent. Then Washington gained thirty pounds so his build would more closely resemble Biko's. As a final touch, he had the caps on his two front teeth changed to reveal the gap between them, similar to the gap in Biko's smile.

In *Cry Freedom*, Washington starred as South African activist Stephen Biko. Kevin Kline, right, played Biko's friend Donald Woods.

When filming began, many felt Washington seemed to become Biko. Donald Woods, who had been a close friend of Biko's for more than ten years, was amazed at Washington's transformation. He later wrote,

> Denzel Washington assumed the Biko personality in his general manner. . . . The skill in his acting was that he did not appear to be acting, but to be behaving as he (Biko) had behaved all his life. [Washington] acquired that quality of stillness, of quiet power, which Biko had had.[3]

"I feel I made a connection with Steve Biko," Washington would later reflect on his performance.[4]

Cry Freedom, released in late 1987, got only moderate attention from the public. Reviews were also often less than favorable. Many critics thought the film lost impact in its effort to balance the two stories of Biko and Woods. Others thought it was a simplistic, stereotypical treatment of Biko's life and apartheid.

Washington, however, received universal praise for his performance. In fact, he was nominated for an Academy Award for Best Supporting Actor. He did not win the honor that year, but it gave him the highest exposure yet to moviegoers and to the industry's directors and producers.

After *Cry Freedom*, Washington turned once again to the theater. This time he was cast in *Checkmates*, by Ron Milner, an accomplished African-American playwright. This was Washington's first chance to act in a Broadway play. In *Checkmates*, Washington played Sylvester

Williams, a liquor distributor in Detroit. Two older, highly respected African-American actors, Ruby Dee and Paul Winfield, shared the stage with Washington. Unfortunately, *Checkmates* did not enjoy a long run.

In 1988, the Washingtons welcomed a daughter, Katia. Pauletta had put her career goals on hold to raise their children, and Denzel was a devoted dad. When asked, he insisted, "Family's always first."[5]

Washington's next project was the British film *For Queen and Country*. Released in 1989, the movie is a dark drama addressing hopelessness in a racist society. Washington starred as Reuben Jones, who returns to south London after fighting for his country in the Falklands War. But Jones's hopes for a life of fair treatment as a black man in a white-dominated society are shattered.

For the movie Washington had to speak with a blended accent—British Cockney and Caribbean. He lived with a family in London for a week to absorb their accent, and then studied with a speech coach.

For Queen and Country got little exposure in the United States, and reviews were generally less than favorable. But for Washington, this was yet another in a growing list of excellent performances. He received consistent praise for the depth and power of his acting.

In another 1989 movie, *The Mighty Quinn*, Washington was again cast as a non-American. Once again, he had to learn a new accent. He worked with a speech coach for six weeks to perfect the cadence and pronunciation of West Indies speech.

Washington's character, Xavier Quinn, is the police chief on a peaceful Caribbean island. He gets along well in the community and is a devoted family man. Then his serene life is shattered when a prominent white businessman is murdered. One of Quinn's best friends becomes the chief suspect. Quinn has to find the murderer, even if it turns out to be his friend.

As with Washington's earlier films, *The Mighty Quinn* did not do well at the box office or with reviewers. But Washington was singled out for his performance. Film critic Roger Ebert predicted Washington's rise to stardom and compared Washington with noted actors Robert Mitchum, Michael Caine, and Sean Connery.[6]

By this time Washington had appeared in six movies. All of them had followed the same pattern: small audiences, lukewarm reviews, and high praise for Washington. For his career to take off, Washington needed to break that pattern. He needed roles in movies that would be seen more widely. That would begin to happen with his next project.

The movie *Glory* is set during the Civil War. It is based on the true story of Colonel Robert Gould Shaw and the first African-American army regiment, which he commanded. Matthew Broderick stars as Shaw. Broderick was well known to audiences at the time for having played the title role in *Ferris Bueller's Day Off*.

In *Glory*, Washington plays the supporting role of Trip, a tough and bitter runaway slave. Normally, Washington refused to play a slave. He thought it was a degrading and undignified stereotype of African Americans. But this movie was different. Explaining his decision later, Washington said, ". . . as long as I feel there is an honest portrayal, a fully realized character, then I would do [the role]."[7]

Glory follows the development of a group of African Americans from widely diverse backgrounds who come together to form the Fifty-fourth Massachusetts Volunteer Infantry. Added to their intense training, they had many obstacles to overcome. The United States Army was reluctant to provide uniforms, shoes, and equal pay for the minority unit. In addition, the men had to fight negative attitudes about their ability to serve. Many people at the time thought African Americans would begin killing whites if given weapons. Others thought they were cowards by nature and would run in fear at the first sound of battle.

The Fifty-fourth proved those fears to be false. The men volunteered for what would become a suicide mission. Surging forward into heavy enemy fire, they made a frontal attack on Battery Wagner, a well-defended fort in South Carolina. Half the unit, including Colonel Shaw, died in that effort.

Trip was a different kind of role for Washington. Up to then, he had usually played intelligent, clean-cut

Washington read old slave journals to immerse himself in the role of a runaway slave who fights in the Civil War. *Glory* was based on the true story of an African-American regiment.

"good guys." But Trip is cynical and a troublemaker, qualities that gave Washington a chance to grow as an actor.

To prepare for the part, Washington spent hours poring over old slave journals to understand life as a slave. Trip was uneducated and spoke in a kind of broken English, another challenge for Washington.[8]

One segment of the movie reveals Trip's character, along with Washington's acting ability. Trip leaves his unit without permission. He is trying to find shoes. When he returns, he is harshly whipped. Trip submits to his punishment as if he were still a slave. Washington plays the scene with a mixture of dignity, resentment, and seething defiance. When the whipping is over, a single tear slowly falls from his cheek. Unplanned by Washington, the tear conveys the hopelessness Trip feels that life will ever get better for blacks in a white society.

Glory was released in 1989 to much publicity and was seen widely by whites as well as African Americans. Critics were generally positive about the movie as well.

For his portrayal of Trip, Washington received the ultimate industry honor—an Academy Award for Best Supporting Actor in a Feature Film. It was a career high point, along with a history-making step forward for African-American actors. Washington was only the second African-American male to win that award. He was delighted. "Winning the Oscar was like jumping

□□□□□□□□□□□□□□□□□□□□□□□□□□□□□□□□□□□□□

into a vat of warm gel," he later said, trying to describe how good it felt to win the award.[9] In addition, Washington received a Golden Globe Award for Best Supporting Actor and an NAACP Image Award. Image Awards are given by the National Association for the Advancement of Colored People to recognize people who have promoted positive portrayals of African Americans.

With his success and growing celebrity from *Glory*, Washington turned next to a film that would get a negative reception from moviegoers and critics. Still, the comedy *Heart Condition* gave him the chance to do lighter material and to expand his talents. Washington plays a successful, elegant lawyer who is murdered. His heart is transplanted into the body of a racist white policeman, played by Bob Hoskins. From there, Washington's ghost helps Hoskins's character solve the murder.

A 1990 release, *Heart Condition* was a box office bomb. Neither audiences nor critics responded well to the movie, and it failed in its attempt to promote racial harmony. Instead, some found it racially offensive.

The same year, Washington teamed up with the prominent African-American director Spike Lee. Lee is a controversial figure, known for his outspoken views. He is a vocal advocate for African-American rights. His films, including *She's Gotta Have It* (1986)

Washington learned some basic trumpeting skills so he would look realistic as a jazz musician in *Mo' Better Blues.*

and *Do the Right Thing* (1989), reflect African-American culture and issues.

Lee's new project, *Mo' Better Blues*, centered on the life of a jazz trumpet player named Bleek Gilliam, played by Washington. Lee based Gilliam on several jazz musicians, including trumpet player Miles Davis. In the movie, Gilliam is driven by his music. He gives little of himself to anything or anyone else.

Again, the role would help Washington depart from his "good guy" image and give him a new acting challenge. To prepare, Washington learned to play the trumpet well enough to appear authentic on screen, although the music was actually played by a professional musician.[10]

In the end, *Mo' Better Blues* did not come together well in most critics' opinions. It received mixed reviews, though Washington was praised for a fine performance.

Also in 1990, Washington set up his own production company. He named it Mundy Lane Entertainment, after his home street in Mount Vernon, New York. One of Mundy Lane's first projects was a documentary film about baseball. Called *Chasing a Dream*, it was shown on the Turner Broadcasting Station (TBS) and received an Emmy Award nomination.

From there, Washington returned to the theater. Anticipating the challenge of another stage role, he said, "Stage is more of an actor's medium. When the lights go up, it's your show. There's no editing process other than the curtain coming down. That's fun."[11]

This time he played the lead in Shakespeare's *Richard III* at New York's Shakespeare Festival. But it turned out to be a surprising failure for Washington. His work was viewed harshly by theater critics.

His next movie, an action thriller called *Ricochet*, appeared in 1991. It was also poorly received. In the film, Washington plays a successful district attorney, Nick Styles, who is pitted against Earl Blake, a killer played by John Lithgow. When Blake is released from prison, he is bent on revenge against Styles, who was responsible for his conviction.

Once the filming was complete, Washington decided he was not cut out to do action movies. Even though in time he would change his mind, he declared this would be his first and last.[12] Audiences and critics were put off by the movie's excessive violence and unlikely action. *Ricochet* received unanimously poor reviews.

Washington's three most recent performances had not been great successes. But this downturn would come to an end with his next movie, *Mississippi Masala*. Washington was so impressed with the script that he agreed to work for one-fourth his normal pay to be in this small-budget film. It is an interracial love story between Washington's character and an Indian woman.

Though *Mississippi Masala* attracted small audiences,

it received top reviews from critics. Washington's performance was applauded as well. The NAACP recognized his work in the film with an Image Award for Outstanding Actor in a Motion Picture.

Washington's career was back on track, and his family was also moving forward. In 1991, he became the father of twins, Malcolm and Olivia.

With his growing celebrity, Washington was getting more and more attention from fans and the media. Rather than bask in the spotlight, he set strict limits, which he has continued to maintain: Denzel Washington keeps his private life private. He rarely agrees to interviews and seldom appears at star-studded events. "I like a low profile," he has said.[13] Shunning the Hollywood limelight, Washington wants to have a normal life. Edward Zwick, who directed him in *Glory*, said of Washington, "Many actors lack a center. He is an authentic person in the world."[14]

Washington's life does not revolve around his work. He sees his career as a way of supporting what is most important to him—his family and his religious faith. He is determined to maintain a healthy family and personal life. Washington wants to give his children the stability of a close, two-parent family that he missed as a teenager.[15]

So, when he is not working, how does Denzel Washington spend his time? Just like any other hands-on dad, Washington is busy shuttling his kids to after-school activities and doctors' appointments, coaching their sports teams, and simply spending time with them.[16] Washington is also devoted to Pauletta. In describing their marriage, he lists "her strength, her friendship, and the way we laugh together" as what he appreciates most.[17] When he is filming, Washington leaves the set each weekend to be with his family.

Even when he is working, Washington maintains his privacy and keeps to himself. For that reason, he has sometimes been viewed as unfriendly by the others on the movie set. But Washington's reclusive style is his way of working. He stays away from cast parties and chatter so he can stay focused on his character.[18]

Washington also gets a great deal of attention from fans because of his famous good looks. Yet he seems unimpressed with his appearance. "Whatever gifts I have been given, I work from the inside out, not from the outside in. I'm not a look. I'm an actor," he has explained.[19]

By the end of 1991, it seemed that Washington was at the peak of his career. He could not know that his success then was just a taste of what was to come.

7

HISTORY COMES TO LIFE

n 1991, after he finished work on *Ricochet*, Washington turned to his next project. It would be a role that many would call his career's best work.

The project had been a long time in planning. For years, Norman Jewison, Washington's director in *A Soldier's Story*, had been thinking of doing a film on the life of Malcolm X. But the project had been delayed. For one thing, many white people had been frightened and offended by Malcolm X's message of black supremacy. And for the movie to be a financial success, it would have to attract white, as well as black, audiences.

After Malcolm X's death, that threat began to soften. By 1991, the time seemed right for the movie.

Malcolm X was one of the most influential African-American leaders in the United States. Born Malcolm Little in 1925 in Omaha, Nebraska, he was the youngest of eight children. His father was a Baptist minister, outspoken in his fight for African-American rights. He was also a strong supporter of Marcus Garvey, an African-American leader who thought African Americans could never achieve equality in the United States and should return to Africa to form a country of their own.

When Malcolm was four years old, his family moved to Michigan. There, the Littles faced bigotry and outright attacks. Soon after their move, the white racist group Black Legion burned their house to the ground while the Littles looked on. Two years later, when Malcolm was six, his father was murdered by racists.

Malcolm's mother tried for six years to keep her large family together. But it became financially impossible. When Malcolm was twelve, his mother had a breakdown and was sent to the state mental hospital. The Little children were split up among several local families.

Two years later, Malcolm moved to Boston, Massachusetts. There he fell in with the African-American underworld. After several unsuccessful attempts at jobs, he turned to crime. He began a life of gambling, dealing drugs, and armed robbery. By the time Malcolm was twenty years old, he had been convicted of robbery and sentenced to ten years in prison.

While in prison, Malcolm learned of a new religion for African Americans. Called the Nation of Islam, it was based on the Muslim faith. It also taught that blacks were God's chosen people, superior to all other races. Whites in particular were deemed "blue-eyed devils" and were considered the enemy. According to Nation of Islam teachings, African Americans would be better off if they completely separated from white society. Its followers called themselves Black Muslims. The religion's founder and leader was the Honorable Elijah Muhammad.

After reading extensively in the prison library about black history and the Islamic faith, Little embraced the Nation of Islam. He devoted his time to learning more about it and became a loyal follower.

Little was released from prison in 1952. He welcomed a fresh start in life as a Black Muslim. As his involvement grew, he eventually became a close adviser to Elijah Muhammad. As part of his faith, he changed his name to Malcolm X. In that way he rid himself of the last name given to his ancestors by whites.

As the years went by, Malcolm became increasingly vocal in his outrage against whites and their treatment of blacks. Whites were responsible for slavery; whites continued to keep the African-American people down. Malcolm X was a powerful, charismatic speaker. "Every time you see a white man, think about the devil you're seeing," he would preach. "Think of how it was on your slave foreparents' bloody, sweaty backs that he built this empire."[1]

Malcolm X attracted many African Americans to the Nation of Islam. Calling for violence against whites if necessary, Malcolm X was seen as a threat to white society. His activities were closely watched by the FBI. His message stood in stark contrast to that of Martin Luther King, Jr., who advocated peaceful coexistence between the races.

Over time, Malcolm X became disenchanted with Elijah Muhammad, his idol for so many years. The Nation of Islam had many strict rules. Malcolm learned of sexual and dietary violations by Elijah Muhammad and began to see him as a fraud to his faith. Malcolm ultimately broke with the Nation of Islam and established his own group, the Muslim Mosque, Inc.

Toward the end of his life, Malcolm X went on a pilgrimage to Mecca in Saudi Arabia. It was a life-changing experience for him. He began to believe that all races, including whites, could live together in peace. But Malcolm X's vision was short-lived. Soon after his return to the United States, he was assassinated.

Many believe his murder had been ordered by Elijah Muhammad.

A movie about the life of Malcolm X would be a major undertaking. It would also be controversial, dredging up strong feelings in whites as well as blacks. But before the project could move forward, the issue of who would direct the movie had to be decided. Norman Jewison had nursed the idea along for years. He intended to be the director.

Hollywood's most outspoken African-American director, Spike Lee, insisted that a white person, even a respected director like Jewison, could not do justice to the film. He explained, "It required a lot of research. . . . The research I'm talking about is talking to the people who knew Malcolm intimately. . . . No way would most of these people open up to someone who was not Black."[2]

Eventually, Lee got his way and became the movie's director. His goal was to make this the first African-American motion picture epic. By the time Lee was put in the director's slot, Washington had already been chosen to play the title role.

For his part, it seemed the natural next step for Washington. Eleven years earlier, after starring in *When the Chickens Come Home to Roost*, Washington had envisioned himself playing Malcolm X again. "Everything I have done as an actor has been in preparation for this," Washington would reflect.[3]

Washington's preparation for *Malcolm X* would be his most rigorous ever. He had already done extensive research for the role in *Chickens*. But now, he wanted to do even more. He read everything he could find that was by, or about, Malcolm X. He watched hours of videotapes so he could learn Malcolm's speech patterns and hand gestures. He talked with members of Malcolm's family, as well as with his friends and enemies. For a time, he also followed the Nation of Islam dietary restrictions of one meal a day. "I just sort of blended into the man as best I could. That was my desire," he said.[4] For Washington, readying himself for the role of Malcolm X came close to obsession.[5]

On top of that, the acting requirements were intense. Washington was in almost every scene of the movie. In all, he would spend a year and a half working on *Malcolm X*. But he was completely committed to the project. It was his most difficult professional challenge yet.

Washington did not necessarily agree with Malcolm X's extreme views. Whereas Malcolm X had, for a time, believed that blacks should separate from whites, Washington's whole career had been geared toward success within a white society. Still, in studying the life of Malcolm X, Washington came to understand the man much better. "My desire, my prayer is for this film to show how a man or a woman can evolve even when

"Everything I have done as an actor has been in preparation for this," said Washington, above, about playing Malcolm X in the movie directed by Spike Lee.

the worst things happen to you, even when you've been taught to hate," Washington said.[6]

Just after beginning work on the film, Washington learned that his father had died. It was a hard blow to handle. But he would incorporate memories of his father's preaching style into his own portrayal of Malcolm X.[7]

Once filming was over, the movie still had problems. Lee was out of money. Running over the movie's $28 million budget by at least $5 million, *Malcolm X* was in danger of never making it into theaters.

But Lee was determined that his movie would be seen. He donated $2 million of his $3 million salary to help cover expenses. That was still not enough. So Lee pleaded the movie's cause to the African-American community's wealthiest and most generous members. Within forty-eight hours, checks started coming in from such celebrities as Bill Cosby, Oprah Winfrey, Magic Johnson, Michael Jordan, and Janet Jackson. The movie would go forward after all.

Ultimately, *Malcolm X* was viewed by wide audiences across racial boundaries. Many were drawn to it because they wanted to learn more about this controversial man. Others wanted to better understand African-American history. Still others saw the movie because of its star, Denzel Washington.

The movie was long—three hours and twenty minutes—which can be a drawback with audiences.

Some moviegoers thought the film portrayed Malcolm X more as a victim of his early life circumstances than as an inflammatory influence on society. But overall, the movie was recognized for its scope and importance. It won the 1992 Berlin Film Festival award for Best Picture. It also was nominated for an Academy Award for Best Picture.

Washington's performance was universally considered nothing short of astonishing.[8] Spike Lee also had the highest praise for Washington's work. He wrote, "For me [Washington as Malcolm X] was more than a likeness. It wasn't superficial, it seemed to come from inside out."[9] Washington's physical transformation into an uncanny likeness of Malcolm X added to the impact.

Reflecting on his performance, Washington said, "I was fortunate enough to be taught as a young actor that it's about the art. . . . The play's the thing. To interpret the work. . . . Not to force the play to my will, not to bend it to make it a Denzel Washington vehicle, but to somewhat lose—and hopefully find—myself in the character and in the work."[10]

Washington received many awards for *Malcolm X*. Among them were the New York Film Critics Circle Award for Best Actor; Best Actor from the Chicago Film Critics; the Silver Bear Award by the Berlin Film Festival; and the Boston Film Critics Association Award for Best Actor. In addition, he was nominated for a Golden Globe and an Academy Award for Best Actor.

Washington lost the Academy Award to Al Pacino for his work in *Scent of a Woman*. He handled the disappointment with grace, saying, "I didn't lose any sleep before or after. It sounds like a stock answer, but it's the truth."[11]

By 1992, it seemed that Washington's career could go no higher. He had been recognized with three Academy Award nominations, winning once for Best Supporting Actor. *People* magazine listed him as one of the "Twenty-Five Most Intriguing People." Whites as well as blacks across the nation admired him and appreciated his excellence in acting. Could life get any better for Denzel Washington?

8

FAME AND FORTUNE

fter completing *Malcolm X*, Washington was exhausted. "It took me quite a while to get back to myself," he admitted.[1] For his next project, he chose much lighter work, taking a minor role as Prince Don Pedro in Shakespeare's *Much Ado About Nothing*.

Shakespeare's play was often performed live in theaters. But Irish actor-director Kenneth Branagh, a longtime Shakespeare buff, wanted to broaden the audience by bringing the play to the movie screen.[2] He chose a powerful group of actors, including Emma

Thompson, Keanu Reeves, Michael Keaton, and Branagh himself.

Washington had already played a number of Shakespearean roles during his career and was happy to participate in Branagh's project. For his part, Branagh was delighted to work with Washington. He later spoke of the actor's "intellectual weight, spiritual gravity, and powerful . . . romantic presence."[3]

The movie was filmed in Italy. It is a tale of mystery, jealousy, and betrayal, with two romantically involved couples at its core. All ends happily, though, with one pair uniting in marriage, and the other soon to follow. Throughout the play, Don Pedro has a key part in making sure everything works out happily.

Although the part of Don Pedro had been written for a white man, Branagh and Washington thought race would not matter. Washington was able to cross racial boundaries and show audiences a new kind of role for an African American.

The movie was released in 1993. Despite Branagh's efforts, *Much Ado About Nothing* was not widely seen by audiences. Washington received mixed reviews for his performance.

That year the Washingtons moved into an English country–style home in Beverly Hills. It had been designed by African-American architect Paul Williams and built in the 1940s. The home has five bedrooms, a guest cottage, and a pool. It had been owned by actor William Holden.

After *Much Ado About Nothing*, Washington was at a crossroads in his career. Each of his movies up to that time had either had an all-African-American cast or been a box office disappointment. Washington needed to star in movies that would get mass exposure among whites as well as blacks. Then he would cross over to being viewed simply as an actor, regardless of his race.

Washington's next two movies boosted him into true celebrity status. The first was *The Pelican Brief*. Based on John Grisham's best-selling novel, the movie also stars Julia Roberts. She had risen to fame with the highly acclaimed movie *Steel Magnolias* (1989) and the wildly popular *Pretty Woman* (1990).

The lead male role in *The Pelican Brief* had been written for a white man. But Washington won the role at Julia Roberts's request. He plays Gray Grantham, an investigative reporter for the *Washington Herald* news-paper. Roberts plays a law student. Their lives intersect in an investigation that begins with the murders of two United States Supreme Court justices. The murders are related, but no one knows why. The justices held opposing political views, and their only connection was their support of environmental issues.

Roberts's character, Darby Shaw, begins to figure out the answer. It involves an oil company's secret and illegal plan to destroy the marshland home of

Louisiana's brown pelicans. Government officials are involved, too, because if they go along with the plan, they will receive huge political contributions. Once they discover that Shaw has uncovered their scheme, her life is in danger. She turns to Grantham as the one person she can trust to help prove and expose the truth.

The Pelican Brief was a box office smash, earning more than $100 million. Although the movie received mixed reviews, the public loved it and its stars. Speaking of Washington's convincing performance, the movie's director, Alan Pakula, commented, "Denzel Washington has the actor's gift of seeming to become what he portrays."[4] *The Pelican Brief* was the perfect crossover follow-up for Washington after his high exposure in *Malcolm X*.

Washington's next movie, *Philadelphia*, costarring Tom Hanks, was released within a week of *The Pelican Brief*. *Philadelphia* was the first major motion picture to address the issue of AIDS. Because of that, it was considered an important movie. Critics were watching closely to see how the movie would treat the difficult issue. Following on the heels of *The Pelican Brief*, it gave audiences another chance to see Washington in a role that crossed racial boundaries.

Washington plays Joe Miller, a successful and aggressive personal injury attorney in Philadelphia. Miller is approached by another lawyer, Andrew

Julia Roberts, right, insisted that Washington be cast as her costar in *The Pelican Brief,* a hit thriller based on a novel by John Grisham.

Beckett, played by Hanks. Beckett has AIDS and needs someone to represent him in a lawsuit against his former employer, who fired him because of his illness.

At first, Miller turns down the case because he is homophobic—fearful of contact with homosexuals. He does not want to work with a homosexual or anyone who has AIDS. Over time, though, Miller changes his mind and takes the case.

By the movie's end, Miller has become more understanding and tolerant. He sees Beckett as a human being, more like himself than different. In summing up the part, Washington later said, "When Joe first meets Andrew, he says, 'Hey, I'm not going to deal with that problem,' but however one is discriminated against, it's wrong and that's something Joe comes around to understanding."[5]

To prepare for the role, Washington spent time with personal injury lawyers. He watched them in action in court to get an idea of how they worked. He also had to get in touch with his feelings about the movie's subject. He told an interviewer, "I want to do everything I can to end AIDS. . . . I don't think I'm like the character (Joe Miller) . . . but . . . it was a good education."[6]

Along with homosexuality and AIDS, the movie deals with the bigger issue of discrimination. It is a problem that Washington, as an African American, has dealt with throughout his life. He has described

In the movie *Philadelphia,* high-powered attorney Joe Miller (Denzel Washington) represents Andrew Beckett (Tom Hanks, left), a gay man with AIDS.

personal experiences with discrimination. "I'm talking about standing in front of a hotel in New York City and watching twenty-eight cabs pass me by. . . . I see women grab their purses when I get on the elevator. . . . So I'm not going to be naive about it. It happens every day."[7]

On the other hand, Washington has learned to deal with the problem. He said, "If you think [racism] limits you, then you are limited, but I don't think that way. All I had to do to get where I am is to work hard."[8]

Philadelphia was seen widely by the public. The movie also received high praise for superb acting and the way it addressed its subject. Tom Hanks won the 1993 Academy Award for Best Actor for his performance. As for Washington, he was pleased with the movie, saying, "This is one of the first films I've been in where I didn't see something I wish wasn't in there."[9]

Washington knew that the combined power of *The Pelican Brief* and *Philadelphia* gave a major boost to his career.[10] At last, he was being seen and accepted by white audiences in white movies. He proved that he could draw moviegoers regardless of race.[11]

Washington's next film, *Crimson Tide*, came out in 1995. The movie takes place in the present, on a submarine. Gene Hackman costars as the submarine's commander, Captain Frank Ramsey. Washington is the second-in-command, Lieutenant Commander Ron

Hunter. Both men have strong personalities, which collide as the plot unfolds.

The suspenseful movie centers on a potential nuclear conflict. Orders for the submarine, the U.S.S. *Alabama*, to fire a nuclear bomb are disrupted as they are being transmitted. So the question is, should they go ahead and launch the attack? Or should they wait until communication resumes and they can confirm the order? Captain Ramsay (Hackman) decides to go ahead with the attack before enemy missiles can be launched against the United States. But to do so he must have Hunter's assistance. And Hunter (Washington) thinks they should wait until they can confirm the order. The rest of the movie is about their struggle for control. It expands to involve the crew, as the men choose sides.

Crimson Tide was another blockbuster for Washington. It was one of the most successful movies of 1995, grossing more than $92 million. The movie, as well as Washington's performance, received glowing reviews. The NAACP honored him with an Image Award for Outstanding Actor in a Motion Picture.

Upon the completion of *Crimson Tide*, Washington began his next project, *Devil in a Blue Dress*. The film, based on a 1990 novel by African-American writer Walter Mosley, is set in the 1940s in Los Angeles. Washington plays the main character, Ezekiel Rawlins, known as "Easy." He is fresh from active duty in World

War II and has settled in Los Angeles in a home of his own. When he is laid off from his job, Easy becomes desperate for money so he can keep his home. He agrees to a quick job as a private investigator, to search for a missing person. But as he gets further into the case, it becomes a murder mystery. Not only is Rawlins himself accused of the murder, his life is endangered as well.

The movie, released in 1995, was the first feature film produced by Washington's Mundy Lane Entertainment. Although it was considered an excellent film by reviewers, it was not seen widely. Washington took the disappointment in stride, saying, "They say period pieces are [a] hard [sell]. . . . But [making a lot of money on a film] is not the criterion for whether it's a good film."[12]

Washington's third project of 1995 was a role in the action thriller *Virtuosity*. In taking the part, he went against his earlier resolution never to do another action movie. The movie also starred rising actor Russell Crowe, who plays a computer-created villain, Sid 6.7, pitted against Washington's character, Parker Barnes.

The movie is set in the near future. It revolves around a plan to train policemen for duty by using computerized villains in a virtual reality setting. But problems arise when Sid 6.7 emerges from the computer and begins terrorizing the public.

Washington plays a former cop who must capture and destroy Sid 6.7.

Washington talked about the difficulties in making the movie: "This was one of the hardest films I've ever done because of the action elements. That was part of the challenge. I've never been in a film where there was so much computer-generated technology. It was an education for me to do this film."[13] Nevertheless, the movie did not attract big audiences and was panned by critics as uninspired and unoriginal.

Washington was ready for a break. "I won't ever again have three pictures out in one year," he said. "It's just too much. . . . That's why I started planning that trip."[14]

The trip he referred to was a monthlong family vacation in Africa. The Washingtons visited the countries of Kenya and Tanzania and the island of Zanzibar. They also went on a camera safari. "I wanted to take the kids on an education vacation," Washington said.[15] They were able to see and film African wildlife.

The family traveled to South Africa as well. It had been eight years since Washington's portrayal of Stephen Biko in *Cry Freedom*. By this time, apartheid had been abolished. The Washingtons were welcomed by the country's president, Nelson Mandela.

The Washingtons also planned another special event for their trip. After twelve years of marriage, Denzel and Pauletta renewed their wedding vows. The ceremony was performed by South Africa's highest religious leader, Archbishop Desmond Tutu.

Washington's next role was as Lieutenant Colonel Nathaniel Serling in the highly acclaimed movie *Courage Under Fire*. He starred with Meg Ryan. The movie is about Serling's search for truth, both in a military investigation and in his own life.

As the movie opens, Serling is commanding a tank crew in a fierce battle in the Persian Gulf. The crew destroys several enemy tanks. Then Serling realizes to his horror that one of the "enemy" tanks they wiped out was actually a United States tank. He is responsible for the deaths of American soldiers, including one of his closest friends.

Throughout *Courage Under Fire*, Serling deals with his guilt. He is also determined to reveal the truth, despite the army's efforts at a cover-up. In addition, Serling is assigned the job of investigating another soldier, played by Meg Ryan. After being killed in the Gulf War, she has been nominated for a Medal of Honor. Washington must find out if the honor is, indeed, deserved.

To prepare for his part, Washington spent time with an M1M1 tank group at the army's National Training Center in Northern California. Besides getting the chance to fire tank artillery, he observed how military people act, move, and think when on duty. He said, "The one thing I kept finding out about these men and women is that they're not just cardboard Rambos. I heard the word integrity used more than ever before. I think we civilians can learn a lot about people in the armed services."[16] Washington hoped the film would highlight the courage of American troops.

Courage Under Fire was a big-budget movie that paid off at the box office. The movie was seen by mass audiences and received excellent reviews. Once again, Washington won accolades from the NAACP, with another Image Award for Outstanding Actor in a Motion Picture. As a special honor, the NAACP also named him Entertainer of the Year.

With *Courage Under Fire* behind him, Washington moved on to a family film. *The Preacher's Wife* would be released during the holiday season of 1996. It was a remake of the 1947 movie *The Bishop's Wife*, with Cary Grant and Loretta Young. Singer-actress Whitney Houston starred with Washington in the updated version.

In a big departure from his many serious roles, Washington would play a charming, easygoing character.[17] "It was a nice change to be able to interact with the crew. Ordinarily I'm off in a corner brooding and preparing for a scene. The scenes here required an equal amount of concentration and preparation, but they were fun," he said.[18]

Washington plays an angel who helps a preacher and his wife (Whitney Houston) rebuild their church

For Washington, playing an angel who helps a preacher and his wife, played by Whitney Houston, left, was an enjoyable change of pace.

and rekindle their marriage. The movie was produced by Washington's Mundy Lane Entertainment and released by Walt Disney Pictures. It was a major undertaking, costing $60 million to produce. It was the highest price tag ever for a movie with an all-black cast.

The Preacher's Wife received mixed reviews. Some found it heartwarming. Others saw it as slow paced and overly sentimental.

Despite the lukewarm reactions to his latest film, Washington's career was soaring. Yet even with all he had accomplished, he somehow managed to keep his feet on the ground. He did not intend to let the success go to his head and said that he did not pay attention to flattering comments. "It's not good to talk about yourself too much," he said.[19]

He also credits his wife, Pauletta, for helping him stay grounded in the real world. "She's like, 'Okay, Mr. Sex Symbol, why don't you try putting some gas in the car.' Reality check!"[20]

Believing that pride would only bring his downfall, Washington said, "When you understand that you are not the reason the sun comes up in the morning, then all these other things you can keep in line. You can remain humble. You see, if you start saying, 'I, Me, I'm The Only One,' it's not going to turn out well for you."[21] After all, Washington says, "Movies are movies. In the end, I go back to being a husband, a son, and a dad."[22]

9

BUILDING ON

SUCCESS

Washington's next movie, *Fallen*, was released in 1998. In this supernatural thriller, he plays a good cop, Detective John Hobbes, who was responsible for the conviction of a serial killer, Edgar Reese. The movie opens with Reese's execution. Soon after the execution, more murders are committed in Reese's signature style. As the mystery unfolds, Hobbes discovers that the evil spirit that caused Reese to kill, lives on. It is passed by touch from person to person. That spirit is bent on destroying Hobbes's career and his life.

"It was a natural for me to take *Fallen* after *The*

Preacher's Wife," Washington told *People* magazine. "I'm sick of being the nice guy."[1] He wanted to get back to a serious role in a more intense film. But *Fallen* did not impress critics. They panned the movie, generally considering it an unconvincing story with a weak script.

Also that year, Washington starred in *He Got Game.* It was his third project with Spike Lee, who wrote, directed, and produced the film. The movie is about the relationship between a father and his son, and the sometimes corrupt world of intercollegiate sports.

Washington plays a supporting role in the movie as Jake Shuttlesworth, an abusive father serving prison time for killing his wife. His son, Jesus, is the nation's number-one high school basketball player. Hundreds of colleges are desperately trying to convince Jesus to sign with them. On top of that, his father (Washington) is offered early parole by the state governor if he can get Jesus to sign with the governor's college.

Washington saw potential in the part of Shuttlesworth. He was ready to stretch his acting muscles once again as a complex, conflicted personality. Jesus was played by Ray Allen, a basketball player for the Milwaukee Bucks.

Not widely seen by audiences, the movie received mixed reviews. Washington's performance was praised along with that of Ray Allen, a newcomer to acting. But overall, the movie's themes were considered jumbled and poorly conveyed. One reviewer said the movie's story had "holes in the plot . . . the size of the Brooklyn Battery Tunnel."[2] Another said, "*He Got Game* piles on issue after issue until the movie weakens under the weight."[3]

Washington's third movie to be released in 1998 was *The Siege*, also starring Bruce Willis and Annette Bening. In it, New York City suffers a series of terrorist attacks. A bus is bombed, along with a federal office building and the theater district. The city comes to a standstill. As FBI Assistant Special Agent Anthony Hubbard, Washington directs the agency's efforts to catch the Islamic terrorists behind the attacks.

The movie drew large audiences but received mixed reviews from critics. Some complained that it suffered because of the simplistic portrayal of the U.S. military as disciplined fanatics.

The following year, 1999, Washington starred in *The Bone Collector*, with actress Angelina Jolie. In this murder mystery, Washington plays Lincoln Rhyme, a brilliant detective. Injured in the line of duty, he is now paralyzed from the neck down. Rhyme has the use of only one index finger, which allows him to operate his wheel chair and computer. He is frustrated and despairing about his future to the point of planning his own suicide. But the New York Police Department needs him to help solve a case. It begins with the disappearance of a multimillionaire and his wife, then evolves into a string of murders by a serial killer.

Playing a quadriplegic presented Washington with another acting challenge. He could not use his body to convey character traits as he was used to doing. During the filming, Washington sometimes had to lie motionless in bed for up to twelve hours at a time. To prepare for the part, he consulted actor Christopher Reeve, a quadriplegic.

Reviews of the film varied. One critic called it "a gimmicky thriller."[4] But Washington's performance met with approval. One reviewer wrote, "Indeed, without moving a limb, [Washington] conveys such a full-blooded conviction about this very average mystery that he carries along everyone he works with."[5]

Washington's five most recent movies had received only halfhearted praise from critics, and he was well aware of the trend. In response, he said, "This is an important and interesting time for me. I've gone all the way around the block, and I've gotten back to the work. Anything that I do now, it's got to be something that I want to do one hundred percent."[6]

Indeed, his next project would be a major film with an interesting and challenging part for him. *The Hurricane* was Washington's second film in 1999. He plays the central character, a middle-weight boxer named Rubin "The Hurricane" Carter.

The film is based on Carter's true-life story. He was wrongly convicted of a triple murder in 1967 and sentenced to life in prison. A group of Canadians became

To portray middle-weight boxer Hurricane Carter, Denzel Washington, above, lost more than forty pounds and learned to box.

convinced of his innocence and worked nineteen years for his release. In 1986, they finally succeeded.

Racism is at the core of the story. Carter was arrested and convicted by a group of racist police and prosecution lawyers aided by the state court's trial judge.

The role gave Washington a chance to portray Carter in many dimensions, first as a cocky young boxer with a bright future. Later, as a prisoner, Carter struggles to deal with his anger and learn to live without hope of release.

Washington's preparation for this role was particularly intense. He had to lose forty-four pounds and undergo strenuous daily workouts to look like Carter. He also had to learn to box convincingly. "If they [the audience] don't buy that, you're done," Washington explained.[7] Altogether, he spent one and a half years with a boxing trainer, preparing for the role.

Although the movie was highly praised by many, it was also criticized for omitting major elements of the true Rubin Carter story. For one thing, it simplified the amount of deception and cover-up used to achieve the boxer's conviction. The movie's defenders argued that some altering of facts was necessary to fit the story into a two-hour film that would keep people interested.

Some thought that racism was underplayed in the movie. One critic wrote, "*The Hurricane* buries the truth in a false Hollywood concoction that blames Rubin's wrongful conviction on one rogue cop."[8]

Yet Washington's portrayal received almost universal acclaim. For example, one reviewer wrote that "whenever Washington is on screen, [the movie] hums with intensity and conviction."[9] Director Norman Jewison similarly praised Washington's performance: "By the end of the film, he was even talking like Hurricane. His phrasing, his pronunciation, his voice itself—it became uncanny."[10] Washington's portrayal would win him a Golden Globe Award for Best Actor, an NAACP Image Award, and an Academy Award nomination for Best Actor.

From *The Hurricane*, Washington rebounded to a family-oriented role as Coach Herman Boone in *Remember the Titans*. The film was released in 2000.

Remember the Titans, based on a true story, takes place in 1971 in Alexandria, Virginia. It shows the painful process of integration at T. C. Williams High School and the task Coach Boone undertook in building a winning football team despite racial tensions.

Washington brought his own experiences as a coach to the role. He had been coaching his children's athletic teams for years. He describes himself as "a motivator more than a taskmaster. . . . I coached younger children . . . so there's not the same pressure to win [as Coach Boone had]."[11] "All I do is tell my kids

Washington's real-life role as coach for his own children's sports teams helped him in his movie role as a football coach in *Remember the Titans.*

they're good. I'm not their best coach, but I'm a good motivator."[12]

In the movie, Washington plays a tough coach who works his team hard. As payoff, they go on to play an undefeated season. The movie attempts to show that racist attitudes can be overcome.

Remember the Titans was criticized for dealing simplistically with integration. Nevertheless, it was enjoyed by wide audiences, thanks to heavy promotion and Washington's box office appeal.

After *Titans* came Washington's award-winning performance as Alonzo Harris in *Training Day*. The movie was released in 2001. At last, after having been nominated five times for an Oscar, Washington became the second African American to win the Academy Award for Best Actor.

Washington's next film was *John Q*, released in 2002. He plays John Q. Archibald, a factory worker whose nine-year-old son needs a heart transplant. Without adequate insurance, the family is unable to pay for the operation. In desperation, Archibald takes the hospital's emergency room hostage at gunpoint and demands that the hospital agree to perform the operation. Only then will he let the hostages go.

Health-care reform is an important issue, and critics applauded the film's subject, but the treatment itself was called overly dramatic and simplistic.

Washington had finally reached the point where

audiences, regardless of race, would pay to see a movie in which he starred. They trusted that it would be worthwhile and that his acting would be superb.[13] Many factors had brought Washington to this place in his career. Talent, dedication, and hard work were at the top of the list. Society was changing, too: Interesting parts for African-American actors were finally opening up. And, of course, there was luck. Or, as Washington himself sums up, success is a result of "the grace of God, the will of man, the hand you're dealt, [and] the way you play it."[14]

10

A Full Life

s Denzel Washington's success grew, he felt an obligation to use some of his resources to help others. Believing that money is to use, rather than to save, he quipped, "I've never yet seen a U-Haul-It trailer attached to a casket."[1] By that he meant you cannot take your money with you when you die, so you might as well use it when you are alive.

Through the years, he has found several outlets for his generosity. One goes back to his boyhood in New York—the Boys and Girls Clubs of America. He has become the organization's national spokesperson. In putting his celebrity behind the club, Washington helps to raise funds and spread the word about its programs.

The Gathering Place, a Los Angeles clinic and shelter for AIDS victims, was also a favorite beneficiary for Washington and his wife. Although it is no longer open, the Washingtons' contributions and efforts to raise money for the shelter kept its doors open for years.

In addition, when meeting with President Nelson Mandela in South Africa, Washington pledged $1 million to the Nelson Mandela Children's Fund. The organization's purpose is to help needy children in that country. About his gift Washington said, "We always give, my wife and I—we believe in that. And this feels right."[2]

Washington has always maintained his faith in God. Despite the time demands of his celebrity, he reads *The Daily Word* (Christian devotions) each morning. His family regularly attends Sunday services at the West Angeles Church of God in Christ—one of the fastest-growing churches in the United States—where they are members. "He's a plain, unassuming person," said his pastor, Bishop Charles E. Blake.[3] Washington pledged $2.5 million toward the church's $50 million building campaign.

Washington has also consistently made his family his number-one priority. He sees them as his anchor.[4]

"Everything you've seen or heard about me, in the media and in the movies, began with lessons I learned to live by at the Club." In thanks, Washington uses his celebrity as national spokesperson for the Boys and Girls Clubs of America.

The actor, who resents the stereotype of the broken black family, tries to have his wife and children with him as much as possible when he is in public. "It's just one small attempt to show that black people can have families," he explained.[5]

The Washingtons moved to a larger home overlooking Beverly Hills in 1997.[6] But rather than putting on fancy airs, Denzel Washington maintains a low-key lifestyle, often wearing comfortable clothes, tennis shoes, and a baseball cap in his off-hours.[7] "Most of our friends are people we've known for years," his wife said. "We've all struggled together. We've all sat on each other's floors . . . [and] eaten out of the same can of Campbell's Chunky Soup. We laugh about it now, but those memories keep us grounded."[8]

A sports nut, Washington has front-row season tickets to the Los Angeles Lakers basketball games. Nevertheless, he rarely uses them anymore. When he does, he is usually hounded by reporters. "I want to see the game, not work," he told *Newsweek* magazine.[9] His one big splurge is on luxury cars, of which he has several.

Washington tries hard to be the best husband and father possible. Besides coaching, he also spends one-on-one time with his children. "I have days with my kids, try to give everybody their special days," he explained.[10] During the summer, he and Pauletta send the children for extended visits with his mother in New York and her parents in North Carolina.

As for his children's futures, Washington expects them all to go to college. In 2002 his older son, John David, won a football scholarship to Morehouse College in Atlanta, Georgia. But after college, it will be their choice what to do with their lives. Washington said, "I'm not putting any pressure on them to be anything except decent individuals and hard-working."[11]

Throughout his career, Washington has drawn continual attention as a sex idol. Named "The Sexiest Man Alive" by *People* magazine in 1996, he appeared on the cover of its July 29 issue. It's something he quickly dismisses. Washington has never wanted to be thought of as just another pretty face. "It doesn't matter how good you look on the screen. If you don't deliver, people aren't going to show up at the theater."[12]

A 1998 Harris Poll listed Washington as America's tenth most popular movie star, male or female. With that, he became the first African-American actor to make the list's top forty.

Despite his overwhelming success and popularity, Washington has not been without criticism. Some have complained that he has chosen only hero or martyr-like (suffering) roles that will earn the public's empathy and loyalty.[13] Others say he has become stereotyped in that way, although his performance in *Training Day* definitely expanded his image.

Washington has also been criticized for his refusal to play explicit romantic scenes in his movies. But he claims that the parts he has played have not lent themselves to that kind of acting. Others suspect that being a devoted family man, the prospect makes him uncomfortable.[14]

Another issue Washington deals with is the complaint by some African Americans that he has betrayed his culture by becoming so successful within white society. But Washington sees it differently. As one writer noted, "On the issue of race, Denzel's personal attitude appears to be that of an old-fashioned Martin Luther King, Jr. integrationist, demanding acceptance as an equal into society at large."[15] Through his ability to rise above color and make it a non-issue to white audiences in films like *Crimson Tide*, *The Pelican Brief*, and *Philadelphia*, Washington makes continued strides against racism, and toward racial equality.

After twenty-seven movies over the past twenty-one years, Denzel Washington shows no sign of slowing down. In the spring of 2002, he started filming *Out of Time*, a thriller for which he earned a reported $20 million. In this movie, scheduled for release in 2003, he plays a police chief in a small Florida town who puts his career on the line for a woman he loves.

Washington was also ready to try his hand at

Denzel Washington and his wife, Pauletta, share the excitement of the 2002 Academy Awards ceremony. In spite of all his success, family is still the first priority for the superstar.

directing a major motion picture. His first project, *Antwone Fisher*, was released at the end of 2002. The movie is based on *Finding Fish*, a memoir by Antwone Fisher, who also wrote the screenplay for the film. An abused and neglected child, Fisher became an angry and violent adult. He went on to join the U.S. Navy and eventually straightened out his life. In the film, Washington plays Fisher's navy psychiatrist. Speaking of the project, Washington said, "[Fisher's] journey is truly a triumph of the spirit, the story of a boy born into circumstances that few of us could withstand, yet who not only survives, but goes on to remarkable success beyond most of our dreams."[16]

Denzel Washington has come a long way from his beginnings in Mount Vernon, New York. He overcame an angry youth, along with a poor start in college, to find his true calling. From there he held fast to his goals, working hard and persevering against racial prejudice. The result? He has become one of the most successful and sought-after actors of his time.

Yet throughout the roller-coaster ride of his career, Washington has stayed true to his values of hard work, devotion to family, and faith in God. Reflecting on his success, Washington said, "It's tough. There's just no way to figure this business out. It's a million-to-one shot, which is why I feel it's so important for me to take full advantage of the opportunities I've been given and fulfill my part of the bargain."[17]

Washington also sees hope for today's up-and-coming African-American actors. He expects them to build on what he has achieved. Referring to the professional "glass ceiling" that can keep people from advancing in their careers, Washington has good advice: "I tell people: the ceiling is glass, not lead. Which means we can break it down."[18] These are words of hope and encouragement from a man who knows what it means to see his dreams come true.

CHRONOLOGY

1954—Denzel Washington is born on December 28 in Mount Vernon, New York.

1968—Enrolls at Oakland Academy in New Windsor, New York.

1969—Parents divorce.

1972—Graduates from Oakland Academy; enters Fordham University.

1977—Meets Pauletta Pearson; graduates from Fordham University; begins studies at the American Conservatory Theater in San Francisco.

1978—Returns to New York City.

1981—Wins Audelco Award for *When the Chickens Come Home to Roost*; wins an Obie Award for *A Soldier's Play*.

1982—Begins role as Dr. Phillip Chandler on television series *St. Elsewhere*.

1983—Marries Pauletta Pearson.

1984—Birth of first son, John David.

1987—Nominated for Academy Award for Best Supporting Actor in *Cry Freedom*.

1988—First daughter, Katia, is born.

1989—Wins Academy Award and Golden Globe for Best Supporting Actor in *Glory*.

1990—Forms Mundy Lane Entertainment.

1991—Twins Malcolm and Olivia are born; Denzel's father dies.

1992—Nominated for Academy Award and Golden Globe for Best Actor for *Malcolm X*; wins Chicago, Boston, and New York film critics' awards for Best Actor; receives Berlin Film Festival Silver Bear Award for Best Actor.

1995—Coproduces *Devil in a Blue Dress*; wins NAACP Image Award for Outstanding Actor in a Motion Picture for *Crimson Tide*.

1996—Wins NAACP Image Award for Outstanding Actor in a Motion Picture for *Courage Under Fire*; NAACP also honors him as Entertainer of the Year.

1998—Named to Harris Poll's list of top ten most popular movie stars.

2000—Wins Golden Globe Award for Best Actor in a Drama for *The Hurricane*; nominated for Academy Award for Best Actor for *The Hurricane*.

2002—Receives Academy Award for Best Actor for *Training Day*.

FILMOGRAPHY

Wilma (television movie), 1977

Flesh and Blood (television movie), 1979

When the Chickens Come Home to Roost (off-Broadway), 1980

A Soldier's Play (off-Broadway), 1980–1981

Carbon Copy, 1981

St. Elsewhere (television series), 1982–1988

License to Kill, 1984

A Soldier's Story, 1984

The George McKenna Story (television movie), 1986

Power, 1986

Cry Freedom, 1987

For Queen and Country, 1989

The Mighty Quinn, 1989

Glory, 1989

Heart Condition, 1990

Mo' Better Blues, 1990

Ricochet, 1991

Mississippi Masala, 1991

Malcolm X, 1992

Much Ado About Nothing, 1993

The Pelican Brief, 1993

Philadelphia, 1993

Crimson Tide, 1995

Devil in a Blue Dress, 1995

Virtuosity, 1995

Courage Under Fire, 1996

The Preacher's Wife, 1996

Fallen, 1998

He Got Game, 1998

The Siege, 1998

The Bone Collector, 1999

The Hurricane, 1999

Remember the Titans, 2000

Training Day, 2001

John Q, 2002

Antwone Fisher, 2002

CHAPTER NOTES

Chapter 1. At the Top

1. Tom O'Neil, *Movie Awards* (New York: Penguin Putnam, Inc., 2001), p. 738.

2. Scott Bowles, "Bad Behavior May Help Washington Win an Oscar," *USA Today*, March 4, 2002, p. 8D.

3. Shep Morgan, "It's Good Cop/Bad Cop, as the White-Hat Actor Delves into the Dark Side," *E! Online*, October 2, 2001.

4. Jay Boyar, "Denzel Washington Plays His First Villain in *Training Day*," Knight-Ridder/Tribune News Service, September 14, 2001.

5. "Denzel Washington, Halle Berry, Will Smith: First Trio of Black Actors to Win Oscar Nominations in 30 Years," *Jet*, March 4, 2002, p. 56.

6. Jessie Carney Smith, *Black Heroes* (Canton, Mich.: Visible Ink Press, 2001), p. 535.

7. Denzel Washington, Academy Award Ceremony, Los Angeles, California, March 24, 2002.

8. Allison Samuels, "Will It Be Denzel's Day?" *Newsweek*, February 25, 2002, p. 57.

Chapter 2. A Strong Beginning

1. David Halberstam, *The Fifties* (New York: Villard Books, 1993), p. x.

2. Lloyd Grove, "A League of His Own," *Vanity Fair*, October 1995, p. 301.

3. Lynn Norment, "Denzel Washington Opens Up About Stardom, Family, and Sex Appeal," *Ebony*, October 1995, p. 34.

4. John Edgar Wideman, "This Man Can Play," *Esquire*, May 1998, p. 72.

5. Jan Janssen, "Dishy Denzel," *McCall's*, July 2000, p. 44.

6. Ed Bradley, *60 Minutes* interview with Denzel Washington, March 31, 2002: "Denzel: A Look into Denzel Washington's Roots," aired July 2, 2000, on CBS-TV.

7. Norment, p. 34.

8. Janssen, p. 44.

9. Grove, p. 299.

10. Pam Lambert, "Heat from a Cool Source," *People Weekly*, July 29, 1996, p. 60.

11. Grove, p. 301.

12. "Denzel Washington: Made for the Part," *Connections*, Spring 1993, p. 14.

13. Douglas Brode, *Denzel Washington: His Films and Career* (Secaucus, N.J.: Birch Lane Press, 1997), p. xv.

14. Norment, p. 34.

15. Rosemary Robotham, "A Love Story: Denzel and Pauletta," *Essence*, December 1996, p. 122.

16. Grove, p. 301.

17. Wideman, p. 72.

18. Bradley.

Chapter 3. The Start of Something Big

1. Elvis Mitchell, "Becoming Biko," *Rolling Stone*, December 3, 1987, p. 32.

2. Lloyd Grove, "A League of His Own," *Vanity Fair*, October 1995, p. 300.

3. Douglas Brode, *Denzel Washington: His Films and Career* (Secaucus, N.J.: Birch Lane Press, 1997), p. xvi.

4. Chris Nickson, *Denzel Washington* (New York: St. Martin's Press, 1996), p. 15.

5. Diane K. Shah, "Soldier, Healer, Seller," *Gentlemen's Quarterly*, October 1988, p. 317.

6. "Denzel Washington and Julia Roberts Star in Probing Suspense Movie 'The Pelican Brief,'" *Jet*, December 20, 1993, p. 58.

7. Christopher J. Farley, "Pride of Place," *Time*, October 2, 1995, p. 72.

8. Rosemary Robotham, "A Love Story: Denzel and Pauletta," *Essence*, December 1996, p. 121.

9. J. C. Trewin, *The Pocket Companion to Shakespeare's Plays* (London: Mitchell Beazley, 1981), p. 119.

10. Nickson, p. 16.

11. "St. Elsewhere Co-Star Started Out to Be M.D." *Jet*, December 3, 1984, p. 55.

12. Douglas Brode, *Denzel Washington: His Films and Career* (Secaucus, N.J.: Birch Lane Press, 1997), p. xviii.

Chapter 4. Slow Going

1. Lloyd Grove, "A League of His Own," *Vanity Fair*, October 1995, p. 246.

2. John Edgar Wideman, "This Man Can Play," *Esquire*, May 1998, p. 69.

3. Ibid.

4. "Negro Ensemble Company," *American Masters*, <http://www.pbs.org> (February 27, 2002).

5. Rosemary Robotham, "A Love Story: Denzel and Pauletta," *Essence*, December 1996, p. 120.

6. Ibid., pp. 120–121.

7. Pam Lambert, "Heat from a Cool Source," *People Weekly*, July 29, 1996, p. 62.

8. Jan Janssen, "Dishy Denzel," *McCall's*, July 2000, p. 43.

9. Laura B. Randolph, "The Glory Days of Denzel Washington," *Ebony*, September 1990, p. 81.

10. Ibid.

11. Laura B. Randolph, "Denzel Washington: The Making of *Malcolm X*," *Ebony*, December 1992, p. 126.

12. Ibid.

Chapter 5. Picking Up Speed

1. Douglas Brode, *Denzel Washington: His Films and Career* (Secaucus, N.J.: Birch Lane Press, 1997), p. xxi.

2. Diane K. Shah, "Soldier, Healer, Seller," *Gentlemen's Quarterly*, October 1988, p. 317.

3. Jan Janssen, "Dishy Denzel," *McCall's*, July 2000, p. 43.

4. David Ansen and Allison Samuels, "In the Eye of 'The Hurricane': Off screen, Denzel Washington Is Grounded," *Newsweek*, January 10, 2000, p. 61.

5. Peter Lev, *American Films of the 70s* (Austin: University of Texas Press, 2000), pp. 127–128.

6. Brode, pp. 23–24.

7. Shah, p. 370.

8. Brode, p. 27.

Chapter 6. The Fast Track

1. Elvis Mitchell, "Becoming Biko," *Rolling Stone*, December 3, 1987, p. 32.

2. Ibid.

3. Donald Woods, *The Making of* Cry Freedom (New York: Henry Holt and Company, 1987), p. 35.

4. Mitchell, p. 32.

5. Laura B. Randolph, "The Glory Days of Denzel Washington," *Ebony*, September 1990, p. 82.

6. Douglas Brode, *Denzel Washington: His Films and Career* (Secaucus, N.J.: Birch Lane Press, 1997), p. 72.

7. Randolph, p. 81.

8. Brode, pp. 76–77.

9. Phoebe Hoban, "Days of Glory," *New York*, August 13, 1990, p. 36.

10. Ibid., p. 37.

11. Ibid., p. 38.

12. Peter Richmond, "Invisible Man: Is Denzel Washington More Than the Sum of His Parts?" *Gentlemen's Quarterly*, January 1994, p. 78.

13. Laura B. Randolph, "Denzel Washington: The Making of *Malcolm X*," *Ebony*, December 1992, p. 125.

14. Richmond, p. 76.

15. Hoban, p. 36.

16. Rosemary Robotham, "A Love Story: Denzel and Pauletta," *Essence*, December 1996, p. 122.

17. Ibid., p. 56.

18. Hoban, p. 38.

19. Lynn Norment, "Denzel Washington Opens Up About Stardom, Family, and Sex Appeal," *Ebony*, October 1995, p. 27.

Chapter 7. History Comes to Life

1. Malcolm X and Alex Haley, *The Autobiography of Malcolm X* (New York: Ballantine Books, 1992), p. 245.

2. Spike Lee, *By Any Means Necessary* (New York: Hyperion, 1992), pp. 32–33.

3. Laura B. Randolph, "Denzel Washington: The Making of *Malcolm X*," *Ebony*, December 1992, p. 125.

4. Ibid., p. 126.

5. Ibid.

6. Lee, p. 116.

7. Lloyd Grove, "A League of His Own," *Vanity Fair*, October 1995, p. 300.

8. Chris Nickson, *Denzel Washington* (New York: St. Martin's Press, 1996), pp. 134–136.

9. Lee, p. 89.

10. Ibid., p. 117.

11. Peter Richmond, "Invisible Man: Is Denzel Washington More Than the Sum of His Parts?" *Gentlemen's Quarterly*, January 1994, p. 137.

Chapter 8. Fame and Fortune

1. Laura B. Randolph, "Denzel Washington: The Making of *Malcolm X*," *Ebony*, December 1992, p. 130.

2. Douglas Brode, *Denzel Washington: His Films and Career* (Secaucus, N.J.: Birch Lane Press, 1997), p. 154.

3. Lloyd Grove, "A League of His Own," *Vanity Fair*, October 1995, p. 246.

4. "Denzel Washington and Julia Roberts Star in Probing Suspense Movie 'The Pelican Brief,'" *Jet*, December 20, 1993, p. 58.

5. "Denzel Washington, Tom Hanks Star in 'Philadelphia' Movie About AIDS," *Jet*, January 31, 1994, p. 55.

6. Peter Richmond, "Invisible Man: Is Denzel Washington More than the Sum of His Parts?" *Gentlemen's Quarterly*, January 1994, p. 78.

7. "Denzel Washington Stars in Military Drama," *Jet*, May 15, 1995, pp. 57, 64.

8. Mal Vincent, "Washington Relishes the Chance to Play a Down-to-Earth Black Hero," Knight-Ridder/Tribune News Service, September 29, 1995.

9. Brendan Lemon, "Brothers," *Interview*, December 1993, p. 90.

10. Chris Nickson, *Denzel Washington* (New York: St. Martin's Press, 1996), pp. 165–166.

11. Ibid.

12. Rebecca Ascher-Walsh, "Uneasy Rider," *Entertainment Weekly*, July 19, 1996, p. 22.

13. "Denzel Washington Tracks Futuristic Killer in New Film 'Virtuosity,'" *Jet*, August 21, 1995, p. 58.

14. Lynn Norment, "Denzel Washington Opens Up About Stardom, Family, and Sex Appeal," *Ebony*, October 1995, p. 34.

15. Grove, p. 299.

16. "Denzel Washington," *Jet*, July 15, 1996, p. 39.

17. "Whitney Houston, Denzel Washington, Courtney B. Vance and Jenifer Lewis Star in 'The Preacher's Wife,'" *Jet*, December 16, 1996, p. 59.

18. Ibid.

19. Laura B. Randolph, "The Glory Days of Denzel Washington," *Ebony*, September 1990, p. 80.

20. Jan Janssen, "Dishy Denzel," *McCall's*, July 2000, p. 43.

21. Spike Lee, *By Any Means Necessary* (New York: Hyperion, 1992), p. 119.

22. Janssen, p. 43.

Chapter 9. Building on Success

1. Leah Rozen, "Fallen from Grace," *People Weekly*, January 26, 1998, p. 138.

2. Stuart Klawans, "He Got Game," *The Nation*, June 1, 1998, p. 35.

3. Leah Rozen, "He Got Game," *People Weekly*, May 4, 1998, p. 31.

4. Ty Burr, "Same Old Serial: Taking its Cue from Moody Thrillers Like *Seven*, *The Bone Collector* Kills Nothing but Time," *Entertainment Weekly*, March 17, 2000, p. 51.

5. Lisa Schwarzbaum, "Piece Keeper," *Entertainment Weekly*, November 12, 1999, p. 53.

6. Cheo Hodari Coker, "Denzel Washington," *Premiere*, December 1999, p. 116.

7. Ed Bradley, *60 Minutes* interview with Denzel Washington, March 31, 2002: "Denzel: A Look into Denzel Washington's Roots," aired July 2, 2000, on CBS-TV.

8. Lewis M. Steel, "Rubin Carter: The Movie," *The Nation*, January 3, 2000, p. 8.

9. David Ansen and Allison Samuels, "In the Eye of 'The Hurricane': Off screen, Denzel Washington Is Grounded," *Newsweek*, January 10, 2000, p. 61.

10. Bruce Fretts, "Denzel Washington: The Hurricane," *Entertainment Weekly*, March 1, 2000, p. 18.

11. Shep Morgan, "The Sexy Titan on Football, Family and Scoring Against the Odds," *E! Online*, September 26, 2000.

12. Peter Richmond, "Invisible Man: Is Denzel Washington More Than the Sum of His Parts?" *Gentlemen's Quarterly*, January 1994, p. 137.

13. "Denzel Washington Is Coach Who Unites Racially Divided Team and Community in 'Remember the Titans,'" *Jet*, October 2, 2000, p. 60.

14. Laura B. Randolph, "The Glory Days of Denzel Washington," *Ebony*, September 1990, p. 82.

Chapter 10. A Full Life

1. Mal Vincent, "Washington Relishes the Chance to Play a Down-to-Earth Black Hero," Knight-Ridder/Tribune News Service, September 29, 1995.

2. Lloyd Grove, "A League of His Own," *Vanity Fair*, October 1995, p. 299.

3. Firooz Zahedi, "Denzel Washington," *People Weekly*, December 28, 1992, p. 45.

4. Janet Cawley, "Denzel Washington: Destined for Greatness," *Biography Magazine*, March 2002, p. 49.

5. Diane K. Shah, "Soldier, Healer, Seller," *Gentlemen's Quarterly*, October 1988, p. 370.

6. Rebecca Ascher-Walsh, "Uneasy Rider," *Entertainment Weekly*, July 19, 1996, p. 20.

7. David Ansen and Allison Samuels, "In the Eye of 'The Hurricane': Off Screen, Denzel Washington Is Grounded," *Newsweek*, January 10, 2000, p. 61.

8. Kim Van Dang, "The Perils of Pauletta," *Ebony*, April 1991, p. 22.

9. Allison Samuels, "Will It Be Denzel's Day?" *Newsweek*, February 25, 2002, p. 58.

10. John Edgar Wideman, "This Man Can Play," *Esquire*, May 1998, p. 72.

11. Lynn Norment, "Denzel Washington Opens Up About Stardom, Family, and Sex Appeal," *Ebony*, October 1995, p. 34.

12. Shep Morgan, "The Sexy Titan on Football, Family and Scoring Against the Odds," *E! Online*, September 26, 2000.

13. Tom Carson, "Denzel's Martyr Complex," *Esquire*, February 2000, p. 64.

14. Pam Lambert, "Heat from a Cool Source," *People Weekly*, July 29, 1996, p. 60.

15. Douglas Brode, *Denzel Washington: His Films and Career* (Secaucus, N.J.: Birch Lane Press, 1997), p. xxvii.

16. Emily Farache, "Denzel Directs!" *E! Online*, April 6, 2001.

17. Khephra Burns, "Denzel," *Essence*, November 1986, p. 132.

18. Ansen and Samuels, p. 61.

FURTHER READING

Brode, Douglas. *Denzel Washington: His Films and Career*. Secaucus, N.J.: Birch Lane Press, 1996.

Hill, Anne E. *Denzel Washington*. Broomall, Pa.: Chelsea House Publishers, 1998.

Nickson, Chris. *Denzel Washington*. New York: St. Martin's Press, 1996.

Wheeler, Jill C. *Denzel Washington*. Minneapolis, Minn.: Abdo, 2002.

INTERNET ADDRESSES

Entertainment Online
<http://www.eonline.com/Facts/People/Bio/0,128,143,00.html>

TV Guide Online. Use the Search feature on this site to get information about Denzel Washington's movies.
<http://www.tvguide.com>

Denzel Washington Photo Gallery
<http://geocities.com/moviefans/denzel.htm>

INDEX

Pages numbers for photographs are in **boldface** type.